ELLEN
WHITE

ON
PREACHING

Insights for
Sharing God's Word

MERVYN A. WARREN

REVIEW AND HERALD® PUBLISHING ASSOCIATION
Since 1861 | www.reviewandherald.com

To order additional copies of *Ellen White on Preaching,*
by Mervyn A. Warren, call **1-800-765-6955**.

Visit us at
www.reviewandherald.com
for information on other Review and Herald® products.

This book was
Edited by Lori Peckham
Copyedited by Lori Peckham
Cover designed by Trent Truman
Cover photo by © 2010 iStock
Typeset: Bembo 11/13

PRINTED IN U.S.A.

14 13 12 11 10   5 4 3 2 1

Library of Congress Cataloging-in-Publication Data
Warren, Mervyn A.
  Ellen White on preaching : insights for sharing God's word / Mervyn A. Warren.
    p. cm.
  Includes index.
  1. Preaching. 2. White, Ellen Gould Harmon, 1827-1915. I. White, Ellen Gould Harmon, 1827-1915. II. Title.
  BV4211.3.W375 2010
  251—dc22
                 2010016903
ISBN 978-0-8280-2553-9

CONTENTS

KEY TO ABBREVIATIONS
of the Writings of E. G. White

AA	*The Acts of the Apostles*
AG	*God's Amazing Grace*
6BC	*The Seventh-day Adventist Bible Commentary*, vol. 6, Ellen G. White Comments
3Bio	*Ellen G. White: The Lonely Years, 1876-1891*, vol. 3
CH	*Counsels on Health*
COL	*Christ's Object Lessons*
CT	*Counsels to Parents, Teachers, and Students*
CW	*Counsels to Writers and Editors*
DA	*The Desire of Ages*
Ed	*Education*
Ev	*Evangelism*
EW	*Early Writings*
FW	*Faith and Works*
GC	*The Great Controversy*
GW	*Gospel Workers*
HP	*In Heavenly Places*
Mar	*Maranatha, the Lord Is Coming*
MB	*Thoughts From the Mount of Blessing*
MH	*The Ministry of Healing*
MM	*Medical Ministry*
9MR	*Manuscript Releases*, vol. 9
OHC	*Our High Calling*
PaM	*Pastoral Ministry*
PK	*Prophets and Kings*
RH	*Review and Herald*
SD	*Sons and Daughters of God*
1SM	*Selected Messages*, book 1
2SM	*Selected Messages*, book 2
ST	*Signs of the Times*
1T	*Testimonies for the Church*, vol. 1 (2T for vol. 2, etc.)
TM	*Testimonies to Ministers and Gospel Workers*
VSS	*The Voice in Speech and Song*

To that great cloud of preachers,
many touching and fueling my homiletic journey
as teachers, students, and pulpit fellows,
lifting aloft the Light of our Lord Jesus Christ.

INTRODUCTION

You already know the imperative. It has been signaling the Christian church for some 2,000 years now. "Preach the Word; be prepared in season and out of season; correct, rebuke and encourage—with great patience and careful instruction" (2 Timothy 4:2, NIV).

First announced in the earliest century A.D. to the apprentice pastor Timothy, this appeal from the itinerant preacher Paul still resounds over the ages, igniting pulpits to declare the gospel of Jesus Christ. Furthermore, Paul's wise admonition lends an appropriate theme and banner for the abundant counsel on preaching by Ellen G. White.

That Paul would urge the preacher to be "prepared" feeds into that branch of homiletic theory that blends spiritual enabling with human endeavor for the preparation and delivery of sermons. In like manner, Ellen White herself consistently encouraged a well-rounded and balanced approach to becoming equipped to "stand in the sacred desk" and "speak the Word of God to the people" (ST, July 28, 1887).

On the more human side of his own personal preparation to accomplish his call to preach, Paul is believed to have been a student and practitioner of public speaking rhetoric prevalent during his time. This may have included learning from ancient Greek and Roman philosophers such as Aristotle, Socrates, and Cicero.

Indeed, some biblical scholars see in the epistles of the apostle evidence that rhetorical principles undergirded his divinely ordained efforts to spread the gospel to both Gentile and Jew. While "God in His providence . . . converted him" (AA 124) and endowed him by the Holy Spirit to preach His Word with power, Paul also brought to the preaching event his background, training, and ability of "matching logic with logic, philosophy with philosophy, eloquence with eloquence" (AA 236).

One well-known Roman instructor in public discourse named Quintilian was a contemporary of Paul. By the second, third, and fourth centuries A.D., the post-New Testament Christian church embraced among its membership converted preachers, exegetes, and scholars who taught that the spiritual call to preach presupposes also appropriate human attention to personal development. Among the most prominent of these converts were Origen (c. 185-254), John Chrysostom (c. 347-407), and Augustine (c. 354-430).

Like an heirloom from the past, this two-dimensional perspective of preaching (divine and human elements working together) found a home also with some early Adventist leaders. Even the inspired pen of Ellen White, tracing her understanding of Bible inspiration as a divine-human experience, seemed to suggest a pattern for preaching the truths of the Bible when she wrote: "The Bible points to God as its author; yet it was written by human hands. . . . The truths revealed are all 'given by inspiration of God' (2 Timothy 3:16); yet they are expressed in the words of men" (GC *v*).

To be sure, all Christian preachers do not believe or adhere to the notion that their preaching activity need bother with any human reliance, and conversely, some go to the opposite pole of considering the pulpit not unlike any social or political speech. Briefly summarized, these are the three main homiletic positions that draw the line in the sand: (1) Preaching is a completely *spiritual* endeavor and needs no dependence on human methodology. (2) Preaching is primarily a *human* activity and differs little, if any, from social, political, or nonworship discourses. (3) Preaching is a *cooperative undertaking* by God and the human instrument.

Reviewing the writings of Ellen White reveals clearly that the process of Bible inspiration and the experience of effective preaching enjoy a kindred cooperative ambience of godly empowerment and dedicated talents, abilities, and training. She balances her admonition that "no one can tell what is lost by attempting to preach without the unction of the

Holy Spirit" (GW 151) with such statements as "I have been shown that there is a decided lack with some who preach the Word. God is not pleased with their ways and ideas. Their haphazard manner of quoting Scripture is a disgrace to their profession. . . . God requires thoroughness of all His servants. . . . Ministers need to be qualified for their position" (2T 501).

Following her numerous articles in the mid-1800s on the need for a competent and prepared ministry, president of the Review and Herald, James White, published: "We are happy to know that the subject of the proper education of men for the ministry is taking strong hold of the minds of our people" (RH, Oct. 23, 1879). He further urged attendance at the biblical and ministerial institute at Battle Creek, whose plans suggested that "one hour each day be devoted to penmanship, one hour to English grammar, and one hour to rhetoric" (3Bio 127). A further announcement pledged a class in elocution (public speaking) by S. S. Hamill, a renowned elocutionist in the United States.

I am proposing that our clergy today in the twenty-first century, and for as long as time shall last, will benefit immensely from inspired counsel on the total package of pulpit preaching. That Ellen White covers such broad boundaries, as well as specific categories, in the formal sharing of the gospel of Jesus Christ never ceases to be amazing. It has been my privilege to draw from her vast reservoir over the past four decades for classes I have taught on college, university, seminary, and graduate-school levels. Please believe me when I affirm that the counsel of Ellen White remarkably covers all the basic principles I have observed from my research of modern authors who supply us with best practices for the pulpit.

To organize some of her selected quotations in this volume, I have chosen the grid of the traditional five canons of rhetoric and public discourse, which are: (1) the *content* of preaching; (2) the *organization* of sermon materials; (3) the *language* of the preacher; (4) the *"memory"* (familiarity) of the preacher with the prepared sermon material; and (5) the *delivery* of the preacher in getting the message across to the congregation. I have added a sixth canon or category based on my observation of something else Ellen White repeatedly calls to our attention: the remaining responsibility the preacher faces *after* the sermon itself has concluded.

If the engine of your preaching could use a comprehensive overhaul and your spirit longs for instructive refreshing on your journey of proclaiming the gospel of salvation, this volume will certainly help along the way.

CHAPTER 1

CONTENT:

The Heart of the Sermon

The heartbeat of preaching has always been energized by its substance, its pith, its essence, its content. According to the theory of preaching, known also as homiletics, sermon content comprises more than just sermon "material" per se, or information alone. Rather, sermon content flows through three arteries of the worship situation: (1) the information or material of the sermon, (2) the preacher, and (3) the audience.

The information or *material* embraces the substance of what the preacher says and how well he or she makes sense of what is being said. Raw material employed by the speaker will come from the Bible and be supported from other sources in the form of narratives or stories (illustrations), examples, quotations, and statistics. As the preacher draws from these sources of evidence (facts and opinions), he or she engages in a process of reasoning that homiletics sometimes calls *logos*. This careful thinking involves *example* reasoning, *analogy* reasoning, *causal* reasoning, or *sign* reasoning, as well as inductive and deductive structures of reasoning. The point here is that when preachers select material for their sermons, they strengthen their preaching when they are able to bring it all together in a communication package that "makes sense" to the congregation.

Some would argue that the *"preacher* material," that is, the personal credibility of the preacher, comprises the most important content in preaching. For sure, the vessel bearing the message carries a most telling influence on whether the sermon will be accepted or rejected. Remember the Roman teacher Quintilian referenced earlier? He called attention to the perceptual oneness of speaker and sermon (or the telling influence of preacher-as-person on the sermon) when he defined public speaking as "a good man speaking well." A more modern communication theorist,

Marshall McLuhan, couches it rather bluntly: "The medium is the message." Preacher Phillips Brooks insists that preaching is "truth through personality"—meaning the authentic self.

I grew up with the idiom "What you do speaks so loudly that I cannot hear what you say." Such an *ethos* stems from the personal character, competence, and goodwill of the preacher, especially as perceived by the hearers.

The third dimension of sermon content resides with the *audience* itself, those who listen and respond to the sermon. Between the pulpit and pew exists an ongoing relational *pathos*. The preacher appeals to the congregation to receive his or her proffered solution to life challenges. The congregation listens to the preacher pointing the way to the good life in Christ. The psychology of preaching says that during the preaching-worship process, an ongoing interaction takes place between pulpit and pew, one that influences each for the success or failure of the experience.

We believe that the Holy Spirit facilitates that experience for the best possible response and outcome for the kingdom of God. The bottom line is that preachers are called to announce good news to real live persons, not straw figures or lifeless mannequins. Furthermore, preachers are encouraged to prepare and shape sermons with specific needs of people in view, thus inducing the preachers to think ahead and analyze the potential makeup and "content" of their audiences. Audience content covers such considerations as age range, gender prominence, professional choices, practical needs, unique desires, and expectations, all in the context of sinners longingly waiting to hear a "word from the Lord."

Preaching Principles of Ellen White on
Sermon Material, Preacher, and *Audience*

Preaching is God's chosen agency. "The preaching of the gospel is God's chosen agency for the salvation of souls. But our first work should be to bring our own hearts into harmony with God, and then we are prepared to labor for others" (5T 87, 88).

Emphasize salvation. "Let the science of salvation be the burden of every sermon, the theme of every song. . . . Bring nothing into your preaching to supplement Christ, the wisdom and power of God" (Ev 185).

Let Daniel and Revelation speak. "Let Daniel speak, let the Revelation speak, and tell what is truth. But whatever phase of the subject is presented, uplift Jesus as the center of all hope, 'the root and the offspring of David, and the bright and morning star'" (TM 118).

10

The lessons of Christ are models for sermons. "The lessons of Christ should be carefully studied, and the subjects, manner, and form of discourses should be modeled after the divine pattern" (RH, June 23, 1891).

Christ drew illustrations from the familiar. "In His teaching, Christ drew His illustrations from the great treasury of household ties and affections, and from nature" (CT 178).

Don't forget the old landmarks. "The passing of the time in 1844 was a period of great events, opening to our astonished eyes the cleansing of the sanctuary transpiring in heaven, and having decided relation to God's people upon the earth, [also] the first and second angels' messages and the third, unfurling the banner on which was inscribed 'the commandments of God, and the faith of Jesus.' One of the landmarks under this message was the temple of God, seen by His truth-loving people in heaven, and the ark containing the law of God. The light of the Sabbath of the fourth commandment flashed its strong rays in the pathway of the transgressors of God's law. The nonimmortality of the wicked is an old landmark. I can call to mind nothing more that can come under the head of the old landmarks. All this cry about changing the old landmarks is all imaginary" (CW 30, 31).

Illustrations should be employed discreetly. "Too many illustrations do not have a correct influence; they belittle the sacred dignity that should ever be maintained in the presentation of the Word of God to the people" (Ev 209).

Christ should be the center. "Put Christ into every sermon. Let the preciousness, mercy, and glory of Jesus Christ be dwelt upon until Christ is formed within, the hope of glory" (RH, March 19, 1895).

Get truth "warm from glory." "I saw that the Spirit of the Lord has been dying away from the church. The servants of the Lord have trusted too much to the strength of argument, and have not had that firm reliance upon God which they should have. I saw that the mere argument of the truth will not move souls to take a stand with the remnant; for the truth is unpopular. The servants of God must have the truth in the soul. Said the angel: 'They must get it warm from glory, carry it in their bosoms, and pour it out in the warmth and earnestness of the soul to those that hear.' A few that are conscientious are ready to decide from the weight of evidence; but it is impossible to move many with a mere theory of the truth. There must be a power to attend the truth, a living testimony to move them" (1T 113).

Mix new themes with old truths. "In every age there is a new development of truth, a message of God to the people of that generation. The old truths are all essential; new truth is not independent of the old, but an unfolding of it. It is only as the old truths are understood that we can comprehend the new" (COL 127).

Choose substance over "smart sermons." "Flowery discourses will not be sufficient to feed the soul of the famishing child of God. The following desire will give a voice to the longing of many a heart that is fed on what are called 'smart sermons.' An intelligent man remarked, 'O that my pastor would give me something besides pretty flowers, and brilliant periods, and intellectual treats! My soul is famishing for the Bread of Life. I long for something simple and nourishing and scriptural.' Daniel Webster gave utterance to these forcible words: 'If clergymen in our day would return to the simplicity of gospel truth, and preach more to individuals and less to the crowd, there would not be so much complaint of the decline of true religion. Many of the ministers of the present day take their text from St. Paul, and preach from the newspapers. When they do so, I prefer to enjoy my own thoughts, rather than listen. I want my pastor to come to me in the Spirit of the gospel, saying, "You are mortal. Your probation is brief, your work must be done speedily. . . . You are hastening to the bar of God. The Judge standeth before the door"'" (PaM 188).

Tell the story of Jesus. "Tell the touching story of His life of self-denial and sacrifice. Tell of His humiliation and death. Tell of His resurrection and ascension, of His intercession for them in the courts of God" (VSS 312).

Preach great themes. "Those who stand before the people as teachers of truth are to grapple with great themes. They are not to occupy precious time in talking of trivial subjects. Let them study the Word, and preach the Word. Let the Word be in their hands as a sharp, two-edged sword. Let it testify to past truths and show what is to be in the future. . . . We are to keep abreast of the time, bearing a clear, intelligent testimony, guided by the unction of the Holy Spirit" (Ev 151).

Christ is our theme. "These are our themes—Christ crucified for our sins, Christ risen from the dead, Christ our intercessor before God; and closely connected with these is the office work of the Holy Spirit, the representative of Christ, sent forth with divine power and gifts for men. His preexistence, His coming the second time in glory and power, His personal dignity, His holy law uplifted, are the themes that have been dwelt upon with simplicity and power" (Ev 187).

Preach righteousness by faith in Christ. "Our churches are dying for the want of teaching on the subject of righteousness by faith in Christ, and on kindred truths" (GW 301).

"When the free gift of Christ's righteousness is not presented, the discourses are dry and spiritless; the sheep and lambs are not fed" (1SM 158).

"All power is given into His hands, that He may dispense rich gifts unto men, imparting the priceless gift of His own righteousness to the helpless human agent. This is the message that God commanded to be given to the world. It is the third angel's message, which is to be proclaimed with a loud voice" (Ev 191).

"Several have written to me, inquiring if the message of justification by faith is the third angel's message, and I have answered, 'It is the third angel's message in verity'" (1SM 372).

"The message of Christ's righteousness is to sound from one end of the earth to the other to prepare the way of the Lord. This is the glory of God, which closes the work of the third angel" (6T 19).

"There is not a point that needs to be dwelt upon more earnestly, repeated more frequently, or established more firmly in the minds of all than the impossibility of fallen man meriting anything by his own best good works. Salvation is through faith in Jesus Christ alone" (FW 19).

The three angels' messages should be repeated. "The proclamation of the first, second, and third angels' messages has been located by the Word of Inspiration. Not a peg or pin is to be removed. . . . It is just as essential now as ever before that they shall be repeated to those who are seeking for the truth" (CW 26).

Make the atonement and cross of Calvary the theme of every sermon. "The cross must occupy the central place because it is the means of man's atonement and because of the influence it exerts on every part of the divine government" (6T 236).

"The cross, the cross of Calvary presented again and again, plainly dwelt upon in every discourse, will prove the life-healing balm, will reveal the beauty and excellence of virtue" (VSS 315).

"Lift Him up, the Man of Calvary, higher and still higher. There is power in the exaltation of the cross of Christ" (Ev 187).

"We are to present Christ and Him crucified, that souls who are dead in trespasses and sins may be alarmed and quickened. . . . Flowery speeches, pleasing tales, anecdotes, and stories do not convict the sinner" (VSS 315).

"The sacrifice of Christ as an atonement for sin is the great truth around which all other truths cluster. In order to be rightly understood and appreciated, every truth in the Word of God, from Genesis to Revelation, must be studied in the light that streams from the cross of Calvary. I present before you the great, grand monument of mercy and regeneration, salvation and redemption—the Son of God uplifted on the cross. This is to be the foundation of every discourse given by our ministers" (GW 315).

"Some ministers err in making their sermons wholly argumentative. There are those who listen to the theory of the truth, and are impressed with the evidences brought out; then, if Christ is presented as the Savior of the world, the seed sown may spring up and bear fruit to the glory of God. But often the cross of Calvary is not presented before the people. Some may be listening to the last sermon they will ever hear, and the golden opportunity, lost, is lost forever. If in connection with the theory of the truth, Christ and His redeeming love had been proclaimed, these might have been won to His side" (GW 158).

"Christ crucified—talk it, pray it, sing it, and it will break and win hearts. . . . The melting love of God in the hearts of the workers will be recognized by those for whom they labor" (RH, June 2, 1903).

"Hanging upon the cross Christ was the gospel. . . . This is our message, our argument, our doctrine, our warning to the impenitent, our encouragement for the sorrowing, the hope for every believer" (6BC 1113).

"Jesus is inviting and drawing by His Holy Spirit the hearts of young and old to Himself. . . . When Christ crucified is preached, the power of the gospel is demonstrated by the influence it exerts over the believer. In place of remaining dead in trespasses and sins, he is awakened. Lift up the Man of Calvary higher and still higher; there is power in the exaltation of the cross of Christ" (SD 221).

"No discourse should ever be preached without presenting Christ and Him crucified as the foundation of the gospel" (GW 158).

Theoretical sermons need a practical application. "Theoretical discourses are essential, that all may know the form of doctrine and see the chain of truth, link after link, uniting in a perfect whole. But no discourse should ever be delivered without presenting Christ and Him crucified as the foundation of the gospel, making a practical application of the truths set forth, and impressing upon the people the fact that the doctrine of Christ is not Yea and Nay, but Yea and Amen in Christ Jesus" (4T 394, 395).

Some preachers confine themselves to a few subjects. "The prophesies and other doctrinal subjects should be thoroughly understood by them all. But some who have been engaged in preaching for years are content to confine themselves to a few subjects, being too indolent to search the Scriptures diligently and prayerfully that they may become giants in the understanding of Bible doctrines and the practical lessons of Christ" (4T 415).

Preaching the new and strange is unnecessary. "Let not our ministers cherish the idea that they must bring forth something new and strange" (Ev 211).

Satan preached the first sermon on the immortality of the soul. "Satan has originated fables with which to deceive. . . . The great original lie which he told to Eve in Eden, 'Ye shall not surely die,' was the first sermon ever preached on the immortality of the soul. That sermon was crowned with success, and terrible results followed. He has brought minds to receive that sermon as truth, and ministers preach it, sing it, and pray it" (1T 342).

There is no need for sensational preaching. "You need not to be sensational. Preach the Word, as Christ, the Son of God, preached the Word" (Ev 184).

Character is more important than words. "There is an eloquence far more powerful than the eloquence of words. . . . What a man is has more influence than what he says" (MH 469).

The love of Christ conquers. "While logic may fail to move, and argument be powerless to convince, the love of Christ . . . may soften the stony heart, so that the seed of truth can take root" (GW 185).

Pulpit efforts are empowered by example. "Ministers should first feel the sanctifying influence of the truth upon their own hearts and in their own lives, and then their pulpit efforts will be enforced by their example out of the desk. Ministers need to be softened and sanctified themselves before God can in a special manner work with their efforts" (3T 237, 238).

Imitate Christ's example. "The servants of Christ should imitate the example of the Master in the manner of labor. They should constantly keep before the people, in the best manner to be comprehended by them, the necessity of practical godliness, and should bring them, as did our Savior in His teachings, to see the necessity of religious principle and righteousness in everyday life. The people are not fed by the ministers of popular churches, and souls are starving for food that will nourish and give spiritual life" (3T 237).

Adapt, not adopt, ideas from others. "The subjects which many of our ministers present before the people are not half as connected and as clear and strong in argument as they should be. They profess to be teachers of the Word, but they sadly neglect to search the Scriptures for themselves. They are content to use the arguments which are prepared in pamphlets and books, and which others have labored earnestly to search out; but they are not willing to tax their minds to study them out for themselves. In order to make full proof of their ministry, those who open the Word of God to others should search the Scriptures diligently. They should not be content to use other men's thoughts, but should dig for truth as for hidden treasures. While it is perfectly right to gather ideas from other minds, they should not be satisfied to take those ideas and repeat them in a poll-parrot manner. Make these ideas your own, brethren; frame the arguments yourselves, from your own study and research. Do not borrow the productions of other men's brains and pens, and recite them as a lesson; but make the most of the talents, the brainpower, that God has given you" (RH, April 6, 1886).

Personal conviction empowers the message. "In this age of moral darkness, it will take something more than dry theory to move souls. Ministers must have a living connection with God. They must preach as if they believe what they say" (GW 151).

The ability to exhort is not enough. "Some have thought that because persons could pray and exhort with a degree of freedom in meeting, they were qualified to go forth as laborers. And before they were proved, or could show any good fruit of their labors, men whom God has not sent have been encouraged and flattered by some brethren lacking experience. But their work shows the character of the workman. They scatter and confuse, but do not gather in and build up. A few may receive the truth as the fruit of their labors, but these generally rise no higher than those from whom they learned the truth. The same lack which marked their own course is seen in their converts" (1T 442).

"A minister may enjoy sermonizing, for it is the pleasant part of the work and is comparatively easy; but no minister should be measured by his ability as a speaker. The harder part comes after he leaves the desk, in watering the seed sown" (5T 255).

Preachers should be Bible students. "Ministers should become Bible students. Are the truths which they handle mighty? Then they should seek to handle them skillfully. Their ideas should be clear and strong, and their spirits fervent, or they will weaken the force of the truth which they handle" (2T 337).

Pastors are shepherds. "Pastors are needed—faithful shepherds—

who will not flatter God's people, nor treat them harshly, but who will feed them with the bread of life" (GW 185).

Some preachers need management. "When a minister is good in the pulpit, and . . . fails in management, he should never go out alone. Another should go with him to supply his lack and manage for him. And although it may be humiliating, he should give heed to the judgment and counsel of this companion, as a blind man follows one who has sight. By so doing he will escape many dangers that would prove fatal to him were he left alone" (1T 442).

Beware of unholy hearts and hands. "It is a fearful thing to minister in sacred things when the heart and hands are not holy. To be a coworker with Christ involves fearful responsibilities; to stand as His representative is no small matter. The fearful realities of the judgment will test every man's work. The apostle [Paul] said, 'We preach not ourselves, but Christ Jesus the Lord;' 'for God, who commanded the light to shine out of darkness, hath shined in our hearts, to give the light of the knowledge of the glory of God in the face of Jesus Christ.' The sufficiency of the apostle was not in himself, but in the gracious influence of the Spirit of Christ, which filled his soul and brought every thought into subjection to the obedience of Christ. The power of truth attending the Word preached will be a savor of life unto life or of death unto death. Ministers are required to be living examples of the mind and spirit of Christ, living epistles, known and read of all men. I tremble when I consider that there are some ministers, even Seventh-day Adventists, who are not sanctified by the truths which they preach. Nothing less than the quick and powerful Spirit of God, working in the hearts of His messengers to give the knowledge of the glory of God, can gain for them the victory.

"Brother B's preaching has not been marked by the sanction of God's Spirit. He can talk fluently and make a point plain, but his preaching has lacked spirituality. His appeals have not touched the heart with a new tenderness. There has been an array of words, but the hearts of his hearers have not been quickened and melted with a sense of a Savior's love. Sinners have not been convicted and drawn to Christ by a sense that 'Jesus of Nazareth passeth by'" (3T 31, 32).

Present truth in an easy style. "In this age, when pleasing fables are drifting upon the surface and attracting the mind, truth presented in an easy style, backed up with a few strong proofs, is better than to search and bring forth an overwhelming array of evidence; for the point then does not stand so distinct in many minds as before the objections and evidences were brought before them. With many, assertions will go further than long arguments. They take many things for granted. Proof does not help the case in the minds of such" (3T 36).

Keep a reserve of arguments. "It is not the best policy to be so very explicit and say all upon a point that can be said, when a few arguments will cover the ground and be sufficient for all practical purposes to convince or silence opponents. You may remove every prop today and close the mouths of objectors so that they can say nothing, and tomorrow they will go over the same ground again. Thus it will be, over and over, because they do not love the light and will not come to the light, lest their darkness and error should be removed from them. It is a better plan to keep a reserve of arguments than to pour out a depth of knowledge upon a subject which would be taken for granted without labored argument. Christ's ministry lasted only three years, and a great work was done in that short period. In these last days there is a great work to be done in a short time. While many are getting ready to do something, souls will perish for the light and knowledge.

"If men who are engaged in presenting and defending the truth of the Bible undertake to investigate and show the fallacy and inconsistency of men who dishonestly turn the truth of God into a lie, Satan will stir up opponents enough to keep their pens constantly employed, while other branches of the work will be left to suffer.

"We must have more of the spirit of those men who were engaged in building the walls of Jerusalem. We are doing a great work, and we cannot come down. If Satan sees that he can keep men answering the objections of opponents, and thus keep their voices silent, and hinder them from doing the most important work for the present time, his object is accomplished" (3T 37, 38).

Preacher sanctification is needed. "Men may present in a clear manner the claims of truth upon others and yet their own hearts be carnal. Sin may be loved and practiced in secret. The truth of God may be no truth to them, because their hearts have not been sanctified by it. The love of the Savior may exercise no constraining power over their base passions. We know by the history of the past that men may stand in sacred positions and yet handle the truth of God deceitfully. They cannot lift up holy hands to God, 'without wrath and doubting.' This is because God has no control over their minds. The truth was never stamped upon their hearts. . . . Their conversion has been only superficial" (5T 536).

Some are excellent in the pulpit, but poor outside of the pul-

pit. "Brother P's success in the ministry, and also in his position of trust in the office, depended upon the character he should maintain. . . . But his own ways have seemed right in his eyes; and he has followed inclination, not heeding the light given him. He was not a safe counselor. He was not a safe man in the office; neither was he a safe shepherd, for he would lead the sheep astray. He has preached excellent discourses; but out of the desk he has not carried out the principles he has preached. This kind of work is an offense to God" (5T 412).

Preach with a sense of solemnity. "Brother B can present arguments upon doctrinal points, but the practical lessons of sanctification, self-denial, and the cross, he has not experienced in himself. He can speak to the ear, but not having felt the sanctifying influence of these truths upon his heart, nor practiced them in his life, he fails to urge the truth home upon the conscience with a deep sense of its importance and solemnity in view of the judgment, when every case must be decided. Brother B has not trained his mind, and his deportment out of meeting has not been exemplary. The burden of the work has not seemed to rest upon him, but he has been trifling and boyish, and by his example has lowered the standard of religion. Sacred and common things have been placed on a level.

"Brother B has not been willing to endure the cross; he has not been willing to follow Christ from the manger to the judgment hall and Calvary. He has brought upon himself sore affliction by seeking his own pleasure. He has yet to learn that his own strength is weakness and his wisdom is folly" (3T 27).

Seek the closet before the pulpit. "The faithful minister of Christ will take the burden upon his soul. He will not hunger after popularity. The Christian minister should never enter the desk until he has first sought God in his closet and has come into close connection with Him. He may, with humility, lift his thirsty soul to God and be refreshed with the dew of grace before he shall speak to the people. With an unction of the Holy Spirit upon him, giving him a burden for souls, he will not dismiss a congregation without presenting before them Jesus Christ, the sinner's only refuge, making earnest appeals that will reach their hearts. He should feel that he may never meet these hearers again until the great day of God" (4T 315, 316).

Your soul must be right before winning souls. "Men whom God has chosen to be His ministers should prepare themselves for the work by thorough heart searching and by close connection with the world's Redeemer. If they are not successful in winning souls to Christ, it is because their own souls are not right with God. There is altogether too much willing ignorance with a large number who are preaching the Word. They are not qualified for this work by a thorough understanding of the Scriptures. They do not feel the importance of the truth for this time, and therefore the truth is not to them a living reality. If they would humble their souls before God; if they would walk according to the Scriptures, in all humility of mind, then they would have more distinct views of the Pattern which they should copy; but they fail to keep their eyes fixed upon the Author and Finisher of their faith" (5T 574).

Practice what you preach. "It is not enough to *preach* the truth; it must be carried out in the life. Christ must be abiding in us, and we in Him, in order to do the work of God. Each must have an individual experience and put forth personal efforts to reach souls. God requires each to put all his powers into the work and, through continual effort, educate himself to do that work acceptably. He expects everyone to bring the grace of Christ into his heart, that he may be a bright and shining light to the world" (5T 576).

Place truth in reach of the audience. "Some have cultivated the habit of too great concentrativeness. The power to fix the mind upon one subject to the exclusion of all others is good to a limited degree, but those who put the whole strength of the mind into one line of thought are frequently deficient on other points. In conversation these become tedious, and weary the listener. Their writings lack a free, easy style. When they speak in public, the subject before them holds their attention, and they are led on and on, to go deeper and deeper into the matter. They seem to see knowledge and light as they become interested and absorbed, but there are few who can follow them.

"There is danger that such men will plant the seed of truth so deep that the tender blade will never find the surface. Even the most essential, manifest truths, those which are of themselves clear and plain, may be so covered up with words as to be made cloudy and indistinct" (GW 169).

There is no place for a loafing preacher. "The Christian ministry is no place for drones. There is a class of men attempting to preach who are slipshod, careless, and irreverent. They would better be tilling the soil than teaching the sacred truth of God" (5T 582).

Proclaim the Word, not fanciful interpretations. "He is to 'preach the word,' not the opinions and traditions of men, not pleasing fables or sensational stories, to move the fancy and excite the emotions. He is not to exalt himself, but as in the presence of God he is to stand before a dying world and preach the Word. There is to be no levity, no trifling, no fanciful interpretation; the minister must speak in sincerity and deep earnestness, as a voice from God expounding the Sacred Scriptures. He is to bring to his hearers those things which most concern their present and eternal good" (GW 147).

Avoid laborious doctrinal reasoning. "Elaborate reasoning or argumentative demonstrations of doctrines seldom impress upon the hearer the sense of his need and his peril" (TM 154).

Place fervent conviction over dry theory. "I feel constrained to say that the labors of many of our ministers lack power. God is waiting to bestow His grace upon them, but they pass on from day to day, possessing only a cold, nominal faith, presenting the theory of the truth, but presenting it without that vital force which comes from a connection with heaven, and which sends the spoken words home to the hearts of men. They are half asleep, while all around them are souls perishing in darkness and error" (GW 35).

Learn from the sermons of Jesus. "In His discourses Christ did not bring many things before them at once, lest He might confuse their minds. He made every point clear and distinct. He did not disdain the repetition of old and familiar truths in prophesies if they would serve His purpose to inculcate ideas" (Ev 56).

Visual aids are helpful. "By the use of charts, symbols, and representations of various kinds, the minister can make the truth stand out clearly and distinctly. This is a help, and in harmony with the Word of God" (GW 355).

There must be neither frivolous joviality nor sourness in the pulpit. "What can the minister do without Jesus? Verily, nothing. Then if he is a frivolous, joking man, he is not prepared to perform the duty laid upon him by the Lord. 'Without me,' says Christ, 'ye can do nothing.' The flippant words that fall from his lips, the trifling anecdotes, the words spoken to create a laugh, are all condemned by the Word of God and are entirely out of place in the sacred desk. . . .

"What is the object of the ministry? Is it to mix the comical with the religious? The theater is the place for such exhibitions. If Christ is formed within, if the truth with its sanctifying power is brought into the inner sanctuary of the soul, you will not have jolly men, neither will you have sour, cross, crabbed men to teach the precious lessons of Christ to perishing souls" (TM 142, 143).

Explanation is better than argument. "Argument is good in its place, but far more can be accomplished by simple explanations of the Word of God" (GW 169).

Practical should be combined with doctrinal. "The practical and the doctrinal should be combined in order to impress hearts with the importance of yielding to the claims of truth after the understanding has been convinced by the weight of evidence" (3T 237).

Preach from a converted heart. "Not all who preach the truth to others are sanctified by it. Some have but faint views of the sacred character of the work. They fail to trust in God and to have all their works wrought in Him. Their inmost souls have not been converted. They have not in their daily life experienced the mystery of godliness. They are handling immortal truths, weighty as eternity, but are not careful and earnest to have these truths inwrought in their souls, made a part of themselves, so that they shall influence them in all they do. They are not so wedded to the principles which these truths inculcate that it is impossible to separate any part of the truth from them.

"Sanctification of heart and life is alone acceptable with God. Said the angel, as he pointed to the ministers who are not right: 'Cleanse your hands, ye sinners; and purify your hearts, ye double minded.' 'Be ye clean, that bear the vessels of the Lord.' God calls for integrity of soul; for truth in the inward parts, transforming the entire man by the renewing of the mind through the influences of the divine Spirit. Not all the ministers are devoted to the work; not all have put their hearts into it. They move as listlessly as though a temporal millennium were allowed them in which to work for souls. They shun burdens and responsibilities, care and privations. Self-denial, suffering, and weariness are not pleasant nor convenient. It is the study of some to save themselves from wearing labor. They study their own convenience and how to please themselves, their wives, and their children; and the work upon which they have entered is nearly lost sight of" (2T 334, 335).

Avoid complicated reasoning. "In Christ's teaching there is no long, far-fetched, complicated reasoning. He comes right to the point" (Ev 171).

Keep your stories to yourself. "Keep your stories to yourself. The people are not soul-hungry for these, but they want the bread of life, the word that liveth and abideth forever. What is the chaff to the wheat?" (Ev 210).

Some preachers do not understand their own messages. "I have been shown that many who profess to have a knowledge of present truth know not what they believe. They do not understand the evidences of their faith. They have no just appreciation of the work for the present time. When the time of trial shall come, there are men now preaching to others who will find, upon examining the positions they hold, that there are many things for which they can give no satisfactory reason. Until thus tested they knew not their great ignorance. And there are many in the church who take it for granted that they understand what they believe; but, until controversy arises, they do not know their own weakness" (5T 707).

"Not all our ministers who are giving the third angel's message really understand what constitutes that message" (5T 715).

Preachers should know Bible exposition. "The one whose special work it is to lead the people into the path of truth should be an able expositor of the Word, capable of adapting his teachings to the wants of the people" (4T 260).

Avoid emotionalism and fanaticism. "With some, religious exercises mean little more than a good time. When their feelings are aroused, they think they are greatly blessed. Some do not think they are blessed unless they are stirred and excited. The intoxication of excitement is the object they are seeking; and if they do not obtain this, they suppose they are all wrong, or that someone else is all wrong.

"People should not be educated to think that religion of an emotional order, bordering on fanaticism, is the only pure religion. Under the influence of such religion the minister is expected to use all his nervous energy in preaching the gospel. He must pour forth with abundance the strong current of the water of life. He must bring stimulating draughts that will be acceptable to human appetite. There are those who, unless their decaying emotions are stimulated, think they can be careless and inattentive" (2SM 21).

The object of preaching is not to entertain. "Men who assume the responsibility of giving to the people the word from the mouth of God make themselves accountable for the influence they exert on their hearers. If they are true men of God, they will know that the object of preaching is not to entertain. It is not merely to convey information, nor to convince the intellect.

"The preaching of the Word should appeal to the intellect and should impart knowledge, but it should do more than this. The minister's utterances, to be effectual, must reach the hearts of his hearers" (GW 152).

The object of preaching is not to amuse. "Neither is it the object of preaching to amuse. Some ministers have adopted a style of preaching that has not the best influence. It has become a habit with them to weave anecdotes into their discourses. The impression thus made upon the hearers is not a savor of life unto life. Ministers should not bring amusing stories into their preaching. The people need pure provender, thoroughly winnowed from the chaff. 'Preach the word' was the charge that Paul gave to Timothy, and this is our commission also. The minister who mixes storytelling with his discourses is using strange fire. God is offended, and the cause of truth is dishonored, when His representatives descend to the use of cheap, trifling words" (TM 318).

Congregations need steps essential for salvation. "Ministers should present the truth in a clear, simple manner. There are among their hearers many who need a plain explanation of the steps requisite in conversion. The great masses of the people are more ignorant on this point than is supposed. Among graduates from college, eloquent orators, able statesmen, men in high positions of truth, there are many who have given their powers to other matters, and have neglected the things of greatest importance. When such men form part of a congregation, the speaker often strains every power to preach an intellectual discourse, and fails to reveal Christ. He does not show that sin is the transgression of the law. He does not make plain the plan of salvation. That which would have touched the hearts of his hearers would have been to point them to Christ dying to bring redemption within their reach" (GW 170).

Feelings aren't true guides. "I saw that the Christian should not set too high a value, or depend too much, upon a happy flight of feeling. These feelings are not always true guides. It should be the study of every Christian to serve God from principle, and not be ruled by feeling. By so doing, faith will be brought into exercise, and will increase" (1T 161).

Christ's disciples assisted. "When the great throngs gathered about the Savior, He would give instruction to the disciples and to the multitude. Then after the discourse the disciples would mingle with the people and repeat to them what Christ had said. Often the hearers had misapplied Christ's words, and the disciples would tell them what the Scriptures said and what Christ had taught that they said" (6T 88).

Arouse the intellect. "Some of the ministers are asleep, and the people are also asleep; but Satan is wide awake. . . . There are ministers preaching present truth who must be converted. Their understanding must be invigorated, their hearts purified, their affections centered in God. They should present the truth in a manner which will arouse the intellect to appreciate its excellence, purity, and sacredness. In order to do this, they should keep before their minds objects which are elevated and which have a purifying, quickening, and exalting influence upon the mind. They must have the purifying fire of truth burning upon the altar of their hearts, to influence and characterize their lives; then, go where they will, amid darkness and gloom, they will illuminate those in darkness with the light dwelling in them and shining round about them.

"Ministers must be imbued with the same spirit as was their Master when He was upon earth. He went about doing good, blessing others with His influence. He was a man of sorrows and acquainted with grief. Ministers should have clear conceptions of eternal things and of God's claims upon them; then they can impress others and excite in them a love for contemplating heavenly things" (2T 336, 337).

Use causal reasoning. "Let our ministers . . . reason from cause to effect" (MM 307).

Some young preachers take sermons of others. "Our young men become self-confident and self-inflated. They take the truths which have been brought out by other minds, and without study or earnest prayer meet opponents and engage in contests, indulging in sharp speeches and witticisms, flattering themselves that this is doing the work of a gospel minister" (4T 446).

Sleeping preachers are preaching to a sleeping people! "By tamely presenting the truth, merely repeating the theory without being stirred by it themselves, they can never convert men. If they should live as long as did Noah, their efforts would be without effect. Their love for souls must be intense and their zeal fervent. A listless, unfeeling manner of presenting the truth will never arouse men and women from their death-like slumber. They must show by their manners, by their acts and words, and by their preaching and praying, that they believe that Christ is at the door. Men and women are in the last hours of probation, and yet are careless and stupid, and ministers have no power to arouse them; they are asleep themselves. Sleeping preachers preaching to a sleeping people!" (2T 337).

Have more teaching, less preaching. "There should be less preaching, and more teaching. There are those who want more definite light than they receive from hearing the sermons. Some need a longer time than do others to understand the points presented" (GW 407).

Don't preach without the Holy Spirit. "No one can tell what is lost by attempting to preach without the unction of the Holy Spirit. In every congregation there are souls who are hesitating, almost decided to be wholly for God. Decisions are being made; but too often the minister has not the spirit and power of the message, and no direct appeals are made to those who are trembling in the balance" (GW 151).

Here is the secret of success. "It is not excitement we wish to create, but deep, earnest consideration, that those who hear shall do solid work, real, sound, genuine work that will be enduring as eternity. We hunger not for excitement, for the sensational; the less we have of this, the better. The calm, earnest reasoning from the Scriptures is precious and fruitful. Here is the secret of success, in preaching a living personal Savior in so simple and earnest a manner that the people may be able to lay hold by faith of the power of the Word of life" (Ev 170).

Remove self. "You will need to be guarded continually to keep self out of sight. You have encouraged a habit of making yourself very prominent. . . . You should forget self and hide behind Jesus. Let the dear Savior be magnified, but lose sight of self. When you see and feel your weakness you will not see that there is anything in yourself worthy of notice or remark. The people have not only been wearied, but disgusted, with your preliminaries before you present your subject. . . .

"You have the example of ministers who have exalted themselves and who have coveted praise from the people. They were petted and flattered by the indiscreet until they became exalted and self-sufficient, and, trusting in their own wisdom, made shipwreck of faith. They thought that they were so popular that they could take almost any course and yet retain their popularity" (3T 235, 236).

A preacher presents arguments; only God converts. "God is not dependent upon any man for the advancement of His cause. He is raising up and qualifying men to bear the message to the world. He can make His strength perfect in the weakness of men. The power is of God. Ready speech, eloquence, great talents, will not convert a single soul. The efforts in the pulpit may stir up minds, the plain arguments may be convincing, but God giveth the increase" (1T 380).

Beware of extremes of audience response. "The religion of many is very much like an icicle—freezingly cold. The hearts of not a few are still unmelted, unsubdued. They cannot touch the hearts of others, because their own hearts are not surcharged with the blessed love that flows from the heart of Christ. There are others who speak of religion as a matter of the will. They dwell upon stern duty as if it were a master ruling with a scepter of iron—a master, stern, inflexible, all powerful—devoid of the sweet, melting love and tender compassion of Christ. Still others go to the opposite extreme, making religious emotions prominent, and on special occasions manifesting intense zeal. Their religion seems to be more of the nature of a stimulus rather than an abiding faith in Christ.

"True ministers know the value of the inward working of the Holy Spirit upon human hearts. They are content with simplicity in religious services. Instead of making much of popular singing, they give their principal attention to the study of the Word, and render praise to God from the heart. Above the outward adorning they regard the inward adorning, the ornament of a meek and quiet spirit. In their mouths is found no guile" (9MR 299, 300).

Focus sermons on audience needs. "You have not been thoroughly furnished from the Word of Inspiration unto all good works. When the flock have needed spiritual food, you have frequently presented some argumentative subject that was no more appropriate for the occasion than an oration upon national affairs. If you would task yourself and educate your mind to a knowledge of the subjects with which the Word of God has amply furnished you, you could build up the cause of God by feeding the flock with food which would be proper and which would give spiritual health and strength as their wants require" (3T 228).

Don't present too much at one time. "My brother, there is danger of your trying to communicate too much at one time. You are not required to make lengthy speeches or to talk upon subjects that will not be understood or appreciated by common people. There is danger of your dwelling upon themes at the very top of the ladder, when those whom you are instructing need to be taught how to climb successfully its first rounds. You talk of things which those unacquainted with our faith cannot comprehend; hence your speeches are not interesting. They are not food for those whom you address" (5T 588).

Avoid cutting and denunciatory sermons. "If Brother White makes one individual feel that he is not doing right, if he is too severe toward that one and needs to be taught to modify his manners, to soften his spirit, how much more necessary for his ministering brethren to feel the inconsistency of making a large congregation suffer from cutting reproofs and strong denunciations, when the really innocent must suffer with the guilty.

"It is worse, far worse, to give expression to the feelings in a large gathering, firing at anyone and everyone, than to go to the individuals who may have done wrong and personally reprove them. The offensiveness of this severe, overbearing, denunciatory talk in a large gathering is of as much more grave a character in the sight of God than giving personal, individual reproof as the numbers are greater and the censure more general. It is ever easier to give expression to the feelings before a congregation, because there are many present, than to go to the erring and, face-to-face with them, openly, frankly, plainly state their wrong course. But bringing into the house of God strong feelings against individuals, and making all the innocent as well as the guilty suffer, is a manner of labor which God does not sanction and which does harm rather than good. It has too often been the case that criticizing and denunciatory discourses have been given before a congregation. These do not encourage a spirit of love in the brethren. They do not tend to make them spiritually minded and lead them to holiness and heaven, but a spirit of bitterness is aroused in hearts. These very strong sermons that cut a man all to pieces are sometimes positively necessary to arouse, alarm, and convict. But unless they bear the especial marks of being dictated by the Spirit of God they do far more injury than they can do good" (3T 507, 508).

Beware of formal worship. "The evil of formal worship cannot be too strongly depicted" (9T 143).

Audience response is good. "There is too much formality in our religious services. The Lord would have His ministers who preach the Word energized by His Holy Spirit; and the people who hear should not sit in drowsy indifference, or stare vacantly about, making no responses to what is said. The impression that is thus given to the unbeliever is anything but favorable for the religion of Christ. These dull, careless professed Christians are not destitute of ambition and zeal when engaged in worldly business; but things of eternal importance do not move them deeply. The voice of God through His messengers may be a pleasant song; but its sacred warnings, reproofs, and encouragements are all unheeded. The spirit of the world has paralyzed them. The truths of God's Word are spoken to leaden ears and hard, unimpressible hearts. . . . Where the church is walking in the light, there will ever be cheerful, hearty responses and words of joyful praise" (5T 318).

Old sermons may not suffice for present audience needs. "God's watchmen must not study how they shall please the people, nor listen to their words and utter them; but they must listen to hear what saith the Lord, what is His word for the people. If they rely upon discourses prepared years before, they may fail to meet the necessities of the occasion. Their hearts should be laid open so that the Lord may impress their minds, and then they will be able to give the people the precious truth warm from heaven" (5T 252).

Too much excitement in worship is uncalled for. "Among most of the colored people we find unseemly practices in their worship of God. They become much excited, and put forth physical exertions that are uncalled for in the solemn worship of God. . . . They conduct their worship according to the instruction they have received, and they think that a religion which has no excitement, no noise, no bodily exercises, is not worth the name of religion" (RH, Dec. 3, 1895). (This statement should be understood in the context of recently liberated and unlearned slaves, as well as immediate descendents of these slaves, in America.)

Don't ride "the chariot of feeling." "Some ministers at the very commencement of a series of meetings become very zealous, take on burdens which God does not require them to bear, exhaust their strength in singing and in long, loud praying and talking, and then are worn out and must go home to rest. What was accomplished in that effort? Literally nothing. The laborers had spirit and zeal, but lacked understanding. They manifested no wise generalship. They rode upon the chariot of feeling, but there was not one victory gained against the enemy. His stronghold was not taken" (1T 647).

Preachers must gain competence. "Mechanics, lawyers, merchants, men of all trades and professions, educate themselves that they may become masters of their business. Should the followers of Christ be less intelligent, and while professedly engaged in His service be ignorant of the ways and means to be employed? The enterprise of gaining everlasting life is above every earthly consideration. In order to lead souls to Jesus there must be a knowledge of human nature and a study of the human mind. Much careful thought and fervent prayer are required to know how to approach men and women upon the great subject of truth.

"Some rash, impulsive, yet honest souls, after a pointed discourse has been given, will accost those who are not with us in a very abrupt manner, and make the truth, which we desire them to receive, repulsive to them. 'The children of this world are in their generation wiser than the children of light.' Businessmen and politicians study courtesy. It is their policy to make themselves as attractive as possible. They study to render their address and manners such that they may have the greatest influence over the minds of those about them. They use their knowledge and abilities as skillfully as possible in order to gain this object.

"There is a vast amount of rubbish brought forward by professed believers in Christ, which blocks up the way to the cross" (4T 67, 68).

Be qualified to preach to the intelligent. "With this class [fanati-

29

cal, ignorant] you have obtained a large share of your religious experience; therefore you are not qualified for the work of teaching the most solemn, refined, elevating, and withal the most testing message to mortals. You may reach a class of minds, but the more intelligent portion of the community will be driven further off by your labors. You have not a sufficient knowledge of even the common branches of education to be an instructor of men and women who have a wily devil on the other hand to suggest and devise ways and means to lead them from the truth. . . .

"It is of infinite importance that all who go forth to teach the truth should be qualified for their work. No less strict investigation should be instituted in reference to their ability to teach the truth than in the case of those who teach our schools. God's work has been belittled by the slack, loose course pursued by professed ministers of Christ.

"I was shown that ministers must be sanctified and holy, and must have a knowledge of the Word of God. They should be familiar with Bible arguments and prepared to give a reason of their hope, or they should cease their labors and engage in a calling where deficiency will not involve such tremendous consequences. Ministers of the popular denominations of the day are acceptable preachers if they can speak upon a few simple points of the Bible; but the ministers who are spreading unpopular truth for these last days, who have to meet men of learning, men of strong minds, and opposers of every type, should know what they are about. They should not take upon themselves the responsibility of teaching the truth unless they are qualified for the work. Before engaging in, or devoting themselves to, the work they should become Bible students. If they have not an education so that they can speak in public with acceptance, and do justice to the truth, and honor the Lord whom they profess to serve, they should wait till they are fitted for the position" (2T 555, 556).

God needs workers to reach the higher classes. "A fund should be raised to educate men and women to labor for these higher classes, both here and in other countries. We have had altogether too much talk about coming down to the common mind. God wants men of talent and good minds, who can weigh arguments, men who will dig for the truth as for hid treasures. These men will be able to reach, not only the common, but the better classes. Such men will ever be students of the Bible, fully alive to the sacredness of the responsibilities resting upon them. They will give proof of their ministry. . . .

"We need the intelligence of varied minds, but we should not find fault with them because their ideas do not just fit our own. We should have broader plans for the education of workers to give the message. . . . [God] calls for cultivated men, who are Bible students, who love the truth that they open to others, and who bring it into their own lives and characters" (5T 580, 581).

Seeking higher education can help reach people. "We would that there were strong young men, rooted and grounded in the faith, who had such a living connection with God that they could, if so counseled by our leading brethren, enter the higher colleges in our land, where they would have a wider field for study and observation. Association with different classes of minds, an acquaintance with the workings and results of popular methods of education, and a knowledge of theology as taught in the leading institutions of learning would be of great value to such workers, preparing them to labor for the educated classes and to meet the prevailing errors of our time. Such was the method pursued by the ancient Waldenses; and, if true to God, our youth, like theirs, might do a good work, even while gaining their education, in sowing the seeds of truth in other minds" (5T 583, 584).

Ministers must never stop learning. "The merchant, the carpenter, the farmer, and the lawyer all have to learn their trade or profession. At first, for want of knowledge, they do imperfect work; but as they continue patiently at their vocations they become masters of their several callings. Without close application of mind and heart, and all the powers of the being, the minister will prove a failure. He may be a preacher, but he must also be fitted to act as a pastor. Study must never cease; it must be continued all through the period of his labor, no matter how well qualified for the labor he may think himself to be.

"The times demand an intelligent, educated ministry, not novices. False doctrines are being multiplied. The world is becoming educated to a high standard of literary attainment; and sin, unbelief, and infidelity are becoming more bold and defiant, as intellectual knowledge and acuteness are acquired. This state of things calls for the use of every power of the intellect; for it is keen minds, under the control of Satan, that the minister will have to meet. He should be well balanced by religious principles, growing in grace and in the knowledge of our Lord Jesus Christ. Too much haphazard work has been done, and minds have not been exercised to their fullest capacity. Our ministers will have to defend the truth against base apostates, as well as to measure Scripture evidence with those who advocate specious errors. Truth must be placed in contrast with bold assertions. Our ministers must be men who are wholly consecrated to God, men of no mean culture;

but their minds must be all aglow with religious fervor, gathering divine rays of light from heaven and flashing them amid the darkness that covers the earth and the gross darkness that surrounds the people" (5T 528).

Young ministers must be educated. "Some young men who enter the field are not successful in teaching the truth to others because they have not been educated themselves. Those who cannot read correctly should learn, and they should become apt to teach before they attempt to stand before the public. The teachers in our schools are not accepted until they have passed a critical examination and their capabilities to teach have been tested by competent judges. No less caution should be used in the examination of ministers" (4T 406).

Successful ministers with little preparation are not the pattern. "Some young men are urging their way into the work who have no real fitness for it. They do not understand that they need to be taught before they can teach. They point to men who, with little preparation, have labored with a measure of success. But if these men were successful, it was because they put heart and soul into the work. And how much more effective their labors might have been if at the first they had received suitable training!" (GW 70).

Continuing education should be sought. "We see the need of encouraging higher ideas of education and of employing more trained men in the ministry. Those who do not obtain the right kind of education before they enter upon God's work are not competent to accept this holy trust and to carry forward the work of reformation. Yet all should continue their education after they engage in the work. They must have the Word of God abiding in them. We need more cultivation, refinement, and nobility of soul in our laborers. Such an improvement as this would show results in eternity" (5T 584).

Reading informs preaching. "Ministers should devote time to reading, to study, to meditation and prayer. They should store the mind with useful knowledge, committing to memory portions of Scripture, tracing out the fulfillment of the prophecies, and learning the lessons which Christ gave to His disciples. Take a book with you to read when traveling on the cars or waiting in the depot. Employ every spare moment in doing something" (4T 412).

Don't rely on feelings, emotions, and sensationalism. "Feelings are often deceiving, emotions are no sure safeguard; for they are variable and subject to external circumstances. Many are deluded by relying on sensational impressions" (4T 188).

Audiences should magnify Christ, not the preacher. "There is too much exhibition of self in the discourses given. Christ crucified, Christ ascended into the heavens, Christ coming again, should so soften, gladden, and fill the mind of the minister of the gospel that he will present these truths to the people in love and deep earnestness. The minister will then be lost sight of and Jesus magnified. The people will be so impressed with these all-absorbing subjects that they will talk of them and praise them, instead of praising the minister, the mere instrument. But if the people, while they praise the minister, have little interest in the word preached, he may know that the truth is not sanctifying his own soul. He does not speak to his hearers in such a manner that Jesus is honored and His love magnified. . . .

"If the praise comes to you, well may you tremble and be ashamed, for the great object is defeated; it is not God, but the servant, that is magnified. Let your light *so shine;* be careful, minister of Christ, in what manner your light shines. If it flashes heavenward, revealing the excellence of Christ, it shines aright. If it is turned upon yourself, if you exhibit yourself, and attract the people to admire you, it would be better for you to hold your peace altogether: for your light shines in the wrong way" (4T 399, 400).

Jesus was sensitive and mindful of His audience. "He spoke as one familiar with heaven, conscious of His relationship to God, yet recognizing His unity with every member of the human family. His messages of mercy were varied to suit His audience. He knew 'how to speak a word in season to him that is weary' (Isa. 50:4); for grace was poured upon His lips, that He might convey to men in the most attractive way the treasures of truth. He had tact to meet the prejudiced minds, and surprise them with illustrations that won their attention. Through the imagination He reached the heart. His illustrations were taken from the things of daily life, and although they were simple, they had in them a wonderful depth of meaning" (DA 254).

Follow the preaching example of the apostles. "The apostles in their preaching went back to Adam's day and brought their hearers down through prophetic history and ended with Christ and Him crucified, calling upon sinners to repent and turn from their sins to God. The representatives of Christ in our day should follow their example and in every discourse magnify Christ as the Exalted One, as all and in all" (4T 401).

Emotional preaching does no lasting good. "It will be seen that those whose minds have the mold of earthliness, those who have a limited Christian experience and know but little of the things of God, are the ones

33

who have the least respect for God's servants and the least reverence for the message He bids them bear. They listen to a searching discourse and go to their homes prepared to sit in judgment on it, and the impression disappears from their minds like the morning dew before the sun. If preaching is of an emotional character, it will affect the feelings, but not the heart and conscience. Such preaching results in no lasting good, but it often wins the hearts of the people and calls out their affections for the man who pleases them. They forget that God has said: 'Cease ye from man, whose breath is in his nostrils'" (5T 301).

Preach with appropriate feeling and fervency. "No one can tell how much is lost by attempting to preach without the unction of the Holy Spirit. There are souls in every congregation who are hesitating, almost persuaded to be wholly for God. The decision is being made for time and for eternity; but it is too often the case that the minister has not the spirit and power of the message of truth in his own heart, hence no direct appeals are made to those souls that are trembling in the balance. The result is that impressions are not deepened upon the hearts of the convicted ones; and they leave the meeting feeling less inclined to accept the service of Christ than when they came. They decide to wait for a more favorable opportunity, but it never comes. That godless discourse, like Cain's offering, lacked the Savior. The golden opportunity is lost, and the cases of these souls are decided. Is not too much at stake to preach in an indifferent manner and without feeling the burden of souls?

"In this age of moral darkness it will take something more than dry theory to move souls. Ministers must have a living connection with God. They must preach as though they believed what they said" (4T 447).

The Holy Spirit reveals the needs of the congregation. "The Spirit of God, if allowed to do its work, will impress the mind with ideas calculated to meet the cases of those who need help. But the tame, formal discourses of many who enter the desk have very little of the vitalizing power of the Holy Spirit in them. The habit of preaching such discourses will effectually destroy a minister's usefulness and ability. . . . God has had too little to do with impressing the mind in the desk" (5T 251, 252).

Preaching is God's chosen method, but not the only means for sharing the gospel. "We are never to forget that Christ teaches through His servants. There may be conversions without the instrumentality of a sermon. Where persons are so situated that they are deprived of every means of grace, they are wrought upon by the Spirit of God and convinced of the truth through reading the Word; but God's appointed means of saving souls is through 'the foolishness of preaching.' Though human, and compassed with the frailties of humanity, men are God's messengers; and the dear Savior is grieved when so little is effected by their labors. Every minister who goes out into the great harvest field should magnify his office" (5T 300).

The sacredness of the sermon is a shield against Satan. "It is Satan's settled purpose to cut off all communication between God and His people, that he may practice his deceptive wiles with no voice to warn them of their danger. If he can lead men to distrust the messenger or to attach no sacredness to the message, he knows that they will feel under no obligation to heed the word of God to them. And when light is set aside as darkness, Satan has things his own way" (5T 300).

Cold formalism must give way to living energy. "The slumbers of those who are lying in sin and error are so deep, so deathlike, that the voice of God through a wide-awake minister is needed to awaken them. Unless the ministers are converted, the people will not be. The cold formalism that is now prevailing among us must give place to the living energy of experimental godliness. There is no fault with the theory of the truth; it is perfectly clear and harmonious. But young ministers may speak the truth fluently, and yet have no real sense of the words they utter. They do not appreciate the value of the truth they present, and little realize what it has cost those, who, with prayers and tears, through trial and opposition, have sought for it as for hid treasures" (4T 445).

Jesus studied faces in the congregation. "Even the crowd that so often thronged His steps was not to Christ an indiscriminate mass of human beings. He spoke directly to every mind and appealed to every heart. He watched the faces of His hearers, marked the lighting up of the countenance, the quick, responsive glance, which told that truth had reached the soul; and there vibrated in His heart the answering chord of sympathetic joy" (Ed 231).

Jesus interacted with and was influenced by His audience. "Jesus watched with deep earnestness the changing countenances of His hearers. The faces that expressed interest and pleasure gave Him great satisfaction. As the arrows of truth pierced to the soul, breaking through the barriers of selfishness, and working contrition, and finally gratitude, the Savior was made glad. When His eye swept over the throng of listeners, and He recognized among them the faces He had before seen, His countenance lighted up with joy. He saw in them hopeful subjects for His kingdom. When the truth, plainly spoken, touched some cherished idol, He marked the change of countenance, the cold, forbidding look, which told that the light was unwelcome. When He saw men refuse the message of peace, His heart was pierced to the very depths" (DA 255).

Arrest the attention of the congregation. "Ministers must be living representatives of the truth they preach. They must have greater spiritual life, characterized by greater simplicity. The words must be received from God and given to the people. The attention of the people must be arrested"(4T 446).

Interesting meetings make acceptable worship. "Our meetings should be made intensely interesting. They should be pervaded with the very atmosphere of heaven. Let there be no long, dry speeches and formal prayers merely for the sake of occupying the time. All should be ready to act their part with promptness, and when their duty is done, the meeting should be closed. Thus the interest will be kept up to the last. This is offering to God acceptable worship. His service should be made interesting and attractive and not be allowed to degenerate into a dry form. We must live for Christ minute by minute, hour by hour, and day by day; then Christ will dwell in us, and when we meet together, His love will be in our hearts, welling up like a spring in the desert, refreshing all, and making those who are ready to perish eager to drink of the waters of life" (5T 609).

The influence of the Spirit is harmonious, not extravagant or coarse. "The progress and perfection of the work of grace in the heart are not dependent upon excitement or extravagant demonstration. Hearts that are under the influence of the Spirit of God will be in sweet harmony with His will. I have been shown that when the Lord works by His Holy Spirit, there will be nothing in its operations which will degrade the Lord's people before the world, but it will exalt them. The religion of Christ does not make those who profess it coarse and rough. The subjects of grace are not unteachable, but ever willing to learn of Jesus and to counsel with one another" (5T 647).

Ministers are influenced by truth preached. "Ministers of the gospel should make the truth of God the theme of study, of meditation, and of conversation. The mind that dwells much on the revealed will of God to man will become strong in the truth. . . .

"There is danger that ministers who profess to believe present truth will rest satisfied with presenting the theory only, while their own souls do not feel its sanctifying power. . . .

"No man is qualified to stand in the sacred desk unless he has felt the transforming influence of the truth of God upon his own soul. Then, and not till then, can he by precept and example rightly represent the life of

Christ. But many in their labors exalt themselves rather than their Master, and the people are converted to the minister instead of to Christ.

"I am pained to know that some who preach the present truth today are really unconverted men. They are not connected with God. They have a head religion, but no conversion of the heart; and these are the very ones who are the most self-confident and self-sufficient; and this self-sufficiency will stand in the way of their gaining that experience which is essential to make them effective workers in the Lord's vineyard" (4T 526, 527).

Ministers are digging their graves with their teeth. "The reason why many of our ministers complain of sickness is that they fail to take sufficient exercise and indulge in overeating. They do not realize that such a course endangers the strongest constitution. Those who, like yourself, are sluggish in temperament should eat very sparingly and not shun physical taxation. Many of our ministers are digging their graves with their teeth. The system, in taking care of the burden placed upon the digestive organs, suffers, and a severe draft is made upon the brain. For every offense committed against the laws of health, the transgressor must pay the penalty in his own body.

"When not actively engaged in preaching, the apostle Paul labored at his trade as a tentmaker" (4T 408, 409).

Ministers must go beyond understanding, believing, and presenting the theory of truth. "The minister may understand and believe the theory of truth, and be able to present it to others; but this is not all that is required of him. 'Faith without works is dead.' He needs that faith that works by love and purifies the soul. A living faith in Christ will bring every action of the life and every emotion of the soul into harmony with God's truth and righteousness.

"Fretfulness, self-exaltation, pride, passion, and every other trait of character unlike our holy Pattern must be overcome; and then humility, meekness, and sincere gratitude to Jesus for His great salvation will continually flow out from the pure fountain of the heart. The voice of Jesus should be heard in the message coming from the lips of His ambassador.

"We must have a converted ministry. The efficiency and power attending a truly converted ministry would make the hypocrites in Zion tremble and sinners afraid. The standard of truth and holiness is trailing in the dust. If those who sound the solemn notes of warning for this time could realize their accountability to God they would see the necessity for fervent prayer" (4T 527, 528).

Be a sermon in shoes. "The religion of Christ, exemplified in the daily life of His followers, will exert a tenfold greater influence than the most eloquent sermons" (4T 547).

Discern Christ, then preach powerfully. "The more clearly ministers discern Christ, and catch His spirit, the more forcibly will they preach the simple truth of which Christ is the center" (Ev 181).

Sermons contribute, but God gives success. "God is not dependent upon any man for the advancement of His cause. He is raising up and qualifying men to bear the message to the world. He can make His strength perfect in the weakness of men. The power is of God. Ready speech, eloquence, great talents, will not convert a single soul. The efforts in the pulpit may stir up minds, the plain arguments may be convincing, but God giveth the increase" (1T 380).

Preliminaries and apologies tire the congregation. "In speaking to the people, he has many apologies to make and many preliminaries to repeat, and the congregation become wearied before he reaches his real subject. As far as possible, ministers should avoid apologies and preliminaries" (2T 670).

Preach repentance and faith. "Many ministers think that it is not necessary to preach repentance and faith, with a heart all subdued by the love of God; they take it for granted that their hearers are perfectly acquainted with the gospel, and that matters of a different nature must be presented in order to hold their attention. If their hearers are interested, they take it as evidence of success. The people are more ignorant in regard to the plan of salvation and need more instruction upon this all-important subject than upon any other" (4T 394).

Audiences need "present truth." "There are many precious truths contained in the Word of God, but it is 'present truth' that the flock needs now" (EW 63).

Amusement threatens conviction. "Amusement is not to be interwoven with instruction in the Scriptures. When this is done, the hearers, amused by some cheap nonsense, lose the burden of conviction" (Ev 211).

Avoid the cheap and the common. "Ministers are to be the mouthpiece of God, and they must eradicate from their speech every expression that is cheap or common. Let them be careful lest by attempting during their discourse to cause laughter, they dishonor God" (Ev 211).

The crisis is now. "Now is the time for the last warning to be given. There is a special power in the presentation of the truth at the present time; but how long will it continue? Only a little while. If there was ever a crisis, it is now" (Ev 16, 17).

CHAPTER 2

ORGANIZATION:

The Eyes of the Sermon

Another term for sermon organization is sermon design. This covers either placing your preaching material into some simple and basic sequence or the more complex task of casting your sermon into one of the more formal designs studied by homiletic classes as "sermon types and forms." One purpose for deliberately shaping your sermon development is the advantage of enabling you as preacher to "see" a plan, a roadmap, for sharing the gospel and also enabling your audience to follow along more easily when traveling with you toward your sermon destination. (After all, no preacher wants to lose his or her hearers due to vague and disarrayed material that confuses more than convinces.)

On the one hand, your sermon can begin with the fundamental approach of merely determining what you will say first, second, third, and so on. On the other hand, you might want to step it up a notch with the more affluent approach of crafting your message according to one of the more reasoned, precise, and tried designs briefly described below. Personally, I have often thought of sermon designing as another means of disclosing the quality of our being created in the image of God. Designing presupposes purpose and foresight and remains one of the most popular and persuasive evidences for the reality of divine existence and activity.

It was Plato who first told us, "A discourse ought to be put together like a living animal, having a head, a body, and a tail." Thus began the age-old and enduring tripartite speaking structure we know as: (a) introduction, (b) body, and (c) conclusion. Other ancient rhetoricians also expressed themselves on the subject. For example, Aristotle averred that public discourse limit itself to no more than four divisions: exordium (introduction), exposition, proof, and peroration (conclusion).

It has been left to homileticians to come up with special organizational developments especially for sermons, a few examples of which are: (1) *Use of points* design—merely numbering your main thoughts in some progressive order. (2) *Interrogative* design—presenting your salient concepts in the form of questions that the sermon proceeds to answer or at least address. (3) *Twin format*—presenting your sermon through two movements, namely "explanation and application," or "data about a Bible personality or experience followed by lessons to be learned," or "description of a Bible narrative or story and the drawing of lessons from that narrative." (4) *Classification* design—dividing people or things into classes and types, which could include the parables of Jesus; the publican and the Pharisee; the wise and foolish virgins; the prodigal son and elder brother; foundations of sand and rock; and types of ground, such as the path, rocky places, thorns, and good soil. (5) *Thematic* design—making use of a striking phrase or line that epitomizes the main idea of the sermon and repeating it intermittently throughout the sermon. A number of sermons by a ministerial friend of mine stand out in my memory, mainly because his oft-repeated thematic refrains still ring in my ears: "Let us make man" and "I am Joseph" and "Earthen vessels are we." Doubtless, the most renowned nonsermonic example in recent times is the "I Have a Dream" speech by Martin Luther King, Jr., delivered at the Lincoln Memorial in 1963. Such a recurring line might originate from your Bible text, some other literary source, or your personal creativity. (6) *Rebuttal* design—staging a refutation of a false and dangerous belief or idea by presenting the concept and asking, "Is this true?" You then answer with scriptural support a resounding "nay."

This is perhaps enough of this parade of possible sermon developments for now. We could, if desired, toss into the hopper of suggested sermon plans Alan Monroe's "motivated sequence" or philosopher G. W. F. Hegel's "thesis-antithesis-synthesis" or the more humanly practical "life situation."

What is our point? Whether or not you employ any of these framed approaches to organizing your sermons, the Ellen White principle of *order* will continue to remain a goal to strive for when preaching the Word of God. Although she herself does not mention any of the preceding "designs," she clearly appealed for sermon organization and counseled preachers to arrange and shape their messages in ways that best facilitate acceptance by the congregation.

Preaching Principles of Ellen White on *Sermon Organization*

Sermons should be clear, connected, and accurate. "Those who teach the Word should not shun mental discipline. Every worker, or company of workers, should by persevering effort establish such rules and regulations as will lead to the formation of correct habits of thought and action. Such a training is necessary not only for the young men but for the older workers, in order that their ministry may be free from mistakes, and their sermons be clear, accurate, and convincing.

"Some minds are more like an old curiosity shop than anything else. Many odd bits and ends of truth have been picked up and stored away there; but they know not how to present them in a clear, connected manner.

"It is the relation that these ideas have to one another that gives them value. Every idea and statement should be as closely united as the links in a chain. When a minister throws out a mass of matter before the people for them to pick up and arrange in order, his labors are lost; for there are few who will do it" (Ev 648, 649).

Sermon design is related to intelligent understanding. "Ministers should . . . have an intelligent understanding of the truth for this time, so that they can give a connected discourse upon the prophesies or upon practical subjects. If they cannot clearly present Bible subjects they need to be hearers and learners still. They should earnestly and prayerfully search the Scriptures, and become conversant with them, in order to be teachers of Bible truth to others. All these things should be carefully and prayerfully considered before men are hurried into the field of labor" (4T 407).

General order must be reflected in the pulpit. "Washington, the nation's statesman, was enabled to perform a great amount of business because he was thorough in preserving order and regularity. Every paper had its date and its place, and no time was lost in looking up what had been mislaid. Men of God must be diligent in study, earnest in the acquirement of knowledge, never wasting an hour. Through persevering exertion they may rise to almost any degree of eminence as Christians, as men of power and influence. But many will never attain superior rank in the pulpit or in business because of their unfixedness of purpose and the laxness of habits. . . . Careless inattention is seen in everything they undertake. . . . If order and regularity are essential in worldly business, how much more so in doing work for God" (4T 411, 412).

Avoid rambling. "Short, plainly made points, avoiding all rambling, will be of the greatest advantage. . . . The speaker must prepare himself for the task. He must not ramble all through the Bible but give a clear, connected discourse, showing that he understands the points he would make" (Ev 181).

CHAPTER 3

LANGUAGE:

The Words of the Sermon

The sermon expresses itself principally, though not entirely, through the medium of words. When viewed in a broader context for our purposes in preaching, language divides itself into three parts: (1) vocabulary, (2) grammar, and (3) creative or symbolic means, usually figures of speech. All three of these elements team up together to distinguish what we call the *style* of the speaker. Lord Chesterfield maintained that style is "the dress of thoughts." Others claim style to be the person herself or himself. At any rate, a typical dictionary definition would say that style is "the mode of expressing thought through language." When ministers face their audiences, they use *words* that supposedly express their understanding of the gospel of Jesus Christ. The challenge is to develop a *vocabulary* that best accomplishes that purpose. Perhaps the more technical route for word study delves into factors of semantics and learns about denotation, connotation, referents, encoding, decoding, and so on along the trail of communication theory. General goals of language in preaching strive for clarity, adaptability, vividness, and forcefulness. For sure, the preacher will keep within arm's reach at least a good dictionary, thesaurus, and other vocabulary-building resources.

Of course, when isolated words are placed in relation to one another to form phrases, clauses, sentences, and paragraphs, the speaker is governed by standards of usage known as *grammar* and *syntax*. As trivial and insignificant as it might sound, those elementary-school playmates called "parts of speech," "subject and verb agreement," "sentence structure," and their other companions do play important parts in preaching the "Word of God."

I have often said to students and practitioners of homiletics that the atonement of Jesus Christ, which is the very best that God could provide for our salvation, certainly deserves our best in the preaching situation—our feeble human words stretching at their best to express the incarnate Word! In order to help keep the preacher growing and improving in this area of correct and effective language usage, a place in his or her library should always be reserved for ready references in grammar for instant assistance and review.

Many preachers I know find it a most refreshing experience to engage in creative ways that express themselves through *symbolic language.* The abiding challenge here is to avoid mistaking the symbol for the substance. (For example, when the gospel writer says that the Holy Spirit descended upon Jesus "like a dove," you as well as your hearers want to understand that the beautiful, creative, imaginative, and meaningful expression "like a dove" does not mean that the Holy Spirit *is* a dove.) The creative symbol may describe and suggest a particular attribute of someone or something, but does not change or determine the substance of that person or object. Christ Himself, as Ellen White says later in this chapter, was a master at clothing truth in creative and figurative language so that His hearers might glimpse a desired aspect of truth expressed in the context of their personal lives.

Our most common communication activity in this area is the use of *figures of speech,* which have been called "the language of power." Although Ellen White is quite positive about the value of creative language, she does not (to my knowledge) *specify* any particular symbolic expressions that preachers should utilize. Nevertheless, we can glean much from her personal practice of using creative language in her own preaching and writing, which offers you and me a treasure trove of examples, a sampling of which are provided later in this chapter.

Preaching Principles of Ellen White on
Sermon Language

People need simple words. "Men and women who spend their lives in humble, commonplace work need words as simple as Christ gave in His lessons, words that are easily understood" (8T 308).

Fluent and correct language is an advantage. "He who knows how to use the English language fluently and correctly can exert a far greater influence than one who is unable to express his thought readily and clearly" (CT 216).

43

Ministry requires overcoming language and speech defects.
"No man should regard himself as qualified to enter the ministry until by persevering effort he has overcome every defect in his utterance" (GW 87).

Christ employed plain language. "Jesus did not employ long and difficult words in His discourses, but used plain language, adapted to the minds of the common people. He ventured no further into the subject He was expounding than they were able to follow Him. . . .

"Many have no idea of the necessity of adapting themselves to circumstances and meeting the people where they are. They do not identify themselves with those whom they wish to help and elevate to the true Bible standard of Christianity" (4T 260, 261).

Christ used familiar symbols. "Christ's manner of teaching was beautiful and attractive, and it was ever characterized by simplicity. He unfolded the mysteries of the kingdom of heaven through the use of figures and symbols with which His hearers were familiar" (CT 240).

Christ clothed cutting truth with figurative language. "In parables He rebuked the hypocrisy and wicked works of those who occupied high positions, and in figurative language clothed truth of so cutting a character that had it been spoken in direct denunciation, they would not have listened to His words, and would speedily have put an end to His ministry" (COL 22).

The language of preachers should not be careless. "Brother E, you cannot fill the position of a minister of Christ. I saw that you lacked a correct religious experience. You have not a knowledge of yourself. You cannot even read correctly, or use language which would commend the truth to the understanding of an intelligent community. You lack discrimination. . . . Your words have been careless" (2T 556, 557).

Cutting, reproving, condemnatory language is inappropriate.
"Some feel that Brother White is altogether too severe in speaking in a decided manner to individuals, in reproving what he thinks is wrong in them. . . . But some of those who complain of his manner of reproving use the most cutting, reproving, condemnatory language, too indiscriminating to be spoken to a congregation. . . . If Brother White makes one individual feel that he is not doing right, if he is too severe toward that one and needs to be taught to modify his manners, to soften his spirit, how much more necessary for his ministering brethren to feel the inconsistency of making a large congregation suffer from cutting reproofs and strong denunciations, when the really innocent must suffer with the guilty" (3T 507).

Christ made truth beautiful through words. "Jesus met the people on their own ground, as one who was acquainted with their perplexities. He made truth beautiful by presenting it in the most direct and simple way. His language was pure, refined, and clear as a running stream" (DA 253).

Both the highly educated and the uneducated understood the words of Christ. "They marveled at the spiritual truth expressed in the simplest language. The most highly educated were charmed with His words, and the uneducated were always profited. He had a message for the illiterate; and He made even the heathen to understand that He had a message for them" (DA 254).

Preaching requires a careful choice of words. "Brother D is too specific. He dwells upon minutiae. He takes time to explain points which are really unimportant and would be taken for granted without producing proof, for they are self-evident. But the real, vital points should be made as forcible as language and proof can make them. They should stand forth as prominent as mileposts. He should avoid many words over little particulars, which will weary the hearer before the important points are reached" (2T 670).

Even the stammering can be eloquent. "Most precious gems of truth are often rendered powerless by the wisdom of words in which they are clothed, while the power of the Spirit of God is lacking. Christ presented the truth in its simplicity; and He reached not only the most elevated, but the lowliest men of earth. The minister who is God's ambassador and Christ's representative on the earth, who humbles himself that God may be exalted, will possess the genuine quality of eloquence. True piety, a close connection with God, and a daily, living experience in the knowledge of Christ, will make eloquent even the stammering tongue" (4T 314).

The Sermon on the Mount had no parade of human eloquence. "When Jesus delivered the Sermon on the Mount, . . . His eyes were lighted up with unutterable love, and the heavenly expression upon His countenance gave meaning to every word uttered. . . . But in these words spoken by the greatest Teacher the world has ever known there is no parade of human eloquence. The language is plain, and the thoughts and sentiments are marked with the greatest simplicity. The poor, the unlearned, the most simple-minded, can understand them. The Lord of heaven was in mercy and kindness addressing the souls He came to save. He taught them as one having authority, speaking the words of eternal life.

"All should copy the Pattern as closely as possible. . . . The messages from heaven are of a character to arouse opposition. The faithful witnesses for Christ and the truth will reprove sin. Their words will be like a hammer to break the flinty heart, like a fire to consume the dross. There is constant need of earnest, decided messages of warning. God will have men who are true to duty. At the right time He sends His faithful messengers to do a work similar to that of Elijah" (5T 253, 254).

Use language eloquent in its simplicity. "They have put tact and skill and knowledge into their work; but how important it is that their hearts, their minds, and all their powers be also trained for faithful service in the cause and worship of God; that they be able to point out the way of salvation through Christ in language eloquent in its simplicity" (5T 409).

Creative Language Used by Ellen White

Although Ellen White speaks of figurative and symbolic language being an asset to preaching (and granting that rhetorical styles are used also by Jesus Christ and biblical writers), as with vocabulary and grammar she states only the basic principles of correct language usage but then leaves the matter with us to study, discover, and practice. We do receive some insight into her own rhetorical choices by observing how she expressed herself. The following sampling of some of her more prominent figures of speech admits us into her special room of literary imaginativeness, which clothed her inspired messages of salvation with beauty, clarity, and appeal for audience understanding and acceptance.

Alliteration: Repetition of the same letter or sound at the beginning of words occurring relatively close together.

"Having put his hand to the plow, he [Elisha] was resolved not to turn back, and through *test* and *trial* he proved *true* to this *trust*" (PK 222).

"Had Elisha allowed the mockery to pass unnoticed, he would have continued to be *ridiculed* and *reviled* by the *rabble,* and his mission to instruct and save in a time of grave national peril might have been defeated" (PK 236).

"He [Jesus] held communion with heaven in song; and as His companions complained of weariness from labor, they were cheered by the sweet melody from His lips. . . . The minds of His hearers were carried away from their *earthly exile,* to the *heavenly home"* (DA 73).

⊙⊘⊙

Anaphora: Repetition of a word or words at the beginning of successive clauses.

"Brother B, *I wish* to alarm you; *I wish* to arouse you to action. *I wish* to entreat of you to seek God while He invites you to come to Him that you may have life" (2T 222).

"*A little longer,* and we shall see the King in His beauty. *A little longer,* and He will wipe all tears from our eyes. *A little longer,* and He will present us 'faultless before the presence of his glory with exceeding joy.' Jude 24" (DA 632).

"God had a work for him [Luther] to do. *He must* yet suffer for the truth. *He must* see it wade through bloody persecutions. *He must* see it clothed in sackcloth and covered with reproach by fanatics. *He must* live to justify it and to be its defender when the mighty powers of earth should seek to tear it down. *He must* live to see it triumph and tear away the errors and superstitions of the papacy" (1T 375).

"There was *no* genuine repentance for sin, *no* contrition, *no* conversion of purpose, *no* abhorrence of evil, and *no* worth or virtue in his [Judas'] confession" (5T 637).

"Souls for whom Christ died are in peril. *So long* as Jesus has said, 'I will never leave thee, nor forsake thee,' *so long* as the crown of righteousness is offered to the overcomer, *so long* as our Advocate pleads in the sinner's behalf, ministers of Christ should labor in hope, with tireless energy and persevering faith" (4T 447).

⊙⊘⊙

Anthropomorphism: Attributing human qualities to God.

"His Spirit is grieved by the pride, extravagance, dishonesty, and over-reaching which are indulged by some professing godliness. All these things bring the *frown* of God upon His people" (4T 491).

❧

Apostrophe: The addressing of a person, usually absent, or a personified thing in an exclamatory and poetic fashion.

"Wonder, O heavens, and be astonished, O earth! Behold the oppressor and the oppressed!" (2T 207). Note her identical expression punctuated differently in another reference: "Wonder, O heavens! and be astonished, O earth! Behold the oppressor and the oppressed" (DA 734).

"O Peter, so soon ashamed of thy Master! so soon to deny thy Lord!" (DA 711).

❧

Asyndeton: Omission of conjunctions to express intensity, vehemence, or speed.

"He who beholds the Savior's matchless love will be elevated in thought, purified in heart, transformed in character. He will go forth to be a light to the world, to reflect in some degree this mysterious love" (DA 661).

"Into all your work you should weave His grace, His love, His devotion, His zeal, His untiring perseverance, His indomitable energy, that will tell for time and for eternity" (4T 603).

"The Word of God is not silent in regard to this momentous time, and it will be understood by all who do not resist His Spirit by determining not to hear, not to receive, not to obey" (5T 719).

"He should toil on, pray on, hope on, amid discouragement and darkness, determined to gain a thorough knowledge of the Scriptures and to come behind in no gift" (4T 447).

"If the future looks somewhat clouded, hope on, believe on" (1T 663).

"When we submit ourselves to Christ, the heart is united with His heart, the will is merged in His will, the mind becomes one with His mind, the thoughts are brought into captivity to Him; we live His life" (COL 312).

໐໐

Eponym: A name so commonly associated with the attributes of its owner that it comes to symbolize those attributes (i.e., Mona Lisa [beauty], Hercules [strength], Croesus [wealth]).

"The Protestant world today see in the little company keeping the Sabbath a *Mordecai* in the gate. His character and conduct, expressing reverence for the law of God, are a constant rebuke to those who have cast off the fear of the Lord and are trampling upon His Sabbath; the unwelcome intruder must by some means be put out of the way" (5T 450).

"At the same time we are to feel entire dependence and trust in God, for we know we cannot do anything without His grace and power to help. *A Paul* may plant, and *an Apollos* water, but God alone can give the increase" (HP 331).

"This you may do; for Enoch pleased Him though living in a degenerate age. And there are *Enochs* in this our day" (COL 332).

໐໐

Historical present: Description of an historical event as if it is taking place in the present, usually by using present-tense verbs, thus giving your audience a sense of "now" rather than a distant "then."

"Evening *is drawing* on as Jesus *calls* to His side three of His disciples,

49

Peter, James, and John, and *leads* them across the fields, and far up a rugged path, to a lonely mountainside. . . .

"Stepping a little aside from them, the Man of Sorrows *pours* out His supplications with strong crying and tears. He *prays* for strength to endure the test in behalf of humanity. . . . And He *pours* out His heart longings for His disciples, that in the hour of the power of darkness their faith may not fail. . . .

"Now the burden of His prayer *is* that they may be given a manifestation of the glory He had with the Father before the world was, that His kingdom may be revealed to human eyes, and that His disciples may be strengthened to behold it. He *pleads* that they may witness a manifestation of His divinity that will comfort them in the hour of His supreme agony with the knowledge that He is of a surety the Son of God and that His shameful death is a part of the plan of redemption.

"His prayer *is* heard. While He is bowed in lowliness upon the stony ground, suddenly the heavens *open*, the golden gates of the city of God *are* thrown wide, and holy radiance *descends* upon the mount, *enshrouding* the Savior's form. Divinity from within *flashes* through humanity, and *meets* the glory coming from above. Arising from His prostrated position, Christ *stands* in godlike majesty. The soul agony is gone. His countenance now *shines* 'as the sun,' and His garments *are* 'white as the light.'

"The disciples, awaking, *behold* the flood of glory that *illuminates* the mount. In fear and amazement they *gaze* upon the radiant form of their Master. . . . Beside Him *are* two heavenly beings, in close converse with Him. They *are* Moses, who upon Sinai had talked with God; and Elijah, to whom the high privilege was given . . . never to come under the power of death. . . . Upon the mount the future kingdom of glory was represented in miniature—Christ the King, Moses a representative of the risen saints, and Elijah of the translated ones" (DA 419-422).

⊘⊘⊘

Litotes: The affirmative is implied by the negative of the opposite (i.e., a variation of saying "The building is big" might be "The building is not small").

"It will be *no unpleasant task* to be obedient to the will of God when we yield ourselves fully to be directed by His Spirit" (3T 378).

"The apostles of nearly all forms of spiritism claim to have power to heal. . . . And there are *not a few,* even in this Christian age, who go to these healers, instead of trusting in the power of the living God and the skill of well-qualified physicians" (PK 211).

"Your only hope now is to make *no feeble move,* but to turn square about. Resolutely call to your aid the willpower that you have so long exercised in the wrong direction, and now work in the opposite direction" (3T 545).

"There are but few good cooks. Young ladies consider that it is stooping to a menial office to become a cook. This is not the case. They do not view the subject from a right standpoint. Knowledge of how to prepare food healthfully, especially bread, is *no mean science*" (1T 682).

≈

Metaphor: An implied comparison or form of expression to overcome abstraction and provide concreteness of meaning through identifying one thing with another that has meaning or connotation familiar to the listener.

"The Lord Jesus has paid your *tuition fees.* All that you have to do is to learn of Him. The Christlike politeness practiced in the *higher school* is to be practiced in this *lower school,* by both old and young believers" (OHC 102).

"The Divine Worker spends little time on worthless material. Only the precious *jewels* does He polish after the similitude of a palace, cutting away all rough edges. This process is severe and trying; it hurts human pride. Christ cuts deep into the experience that man in his self-sufficiency has regarded as complete and takes away self-uplifting from the character. He cuts away the surplus surface, and putting the *stone* to the *polishing wheel,* presses it close, that all roughness may be worn away. Then, holding the *jewel* up to the light, the Master sees in it a reflection of Himself, and He pronounces it worthy of a place in His *casket.* Blessed be the experience, however severe, that gives new value to the *stone*" (HP 267).

"The *oil of grace* should be in *our vessels* with *our lamps.* . . . Why has

51

the Lord so long delayed His coming? The whole host of heaven is waiting to fulfill the last work for this lost world, and yet the work waits. It is because the few who profess to have the *oil of grace* in *their vessels* with *their lamps* have not become burning and shining lights in the world. . . . Then see that you have the *oil of grace* in your hearts" (Mar 55).

"Do not settle down in *Satan's easy chair*, and say that there is no use, you cannot cease to sin, that there is no power in you to overcome. There is no power in you apart from Christ, but it is your privilege to have Christ abiding in your heart by faith, and He can overcome sin in you, when you cooperate with His efforts" (OHC 76).

"Are there not many unpleasant pictures hanging in memory's halls?" (5T 610).

"A man may have precious *seed* in his hand, but that *seed* is not an *orchard*. The *seed* must be planted before it can become a *tree*. The *mind* is the *garden*; the *character* is the *fruit*. God has given us our faculties to cultivate and develop. Our own course determines our character" (4T 606).

"Much time should be spent in prayer, that our *garments of character* may be washed and made white in the blood of the Lamb" (5T 717).

"Never hide *your colors*, never put *your light* under a *bushel* or under a *bed*, but set it on a *candlestick*, that it may give *light* to all that are in the *house*" (5T 588).

"Your worldliness does not incline you to throw wide open the *door of your hard hearts* at the knock of Jesus, who is seeking an entrance there. The Lord of glory, who has redeemed you by His own blood, waited at *your doors* for admittance; but you did not throw them open wide and welcome Him in. Some *opened the door* slightly and permitted a little *light* from His presence to enter, but did not welcome the heavenly Visitor. There was not room for Jesus. The place which should have been reserved for Him was occupied with other things. . . . There was a work for you to do to *open the door*. . . . Some, however, *opened the door* and heartily welcomed their Savior" (2T 216, 217).

⋐⋑

Paronomasia: Setting in close proximity to each other words that are similar in sound.

"The cross of Christ will be the science and the song of the redeemed through all eternity. In Christ *glorified* they will behold Christ *crucified*" (GC 651).

"Satan is the *destroyer*, Christ the *restorer*" (AG 147).

"It may seem that we are to study our own hearts, and square our own actions by some standard of our own; but this is not the case. This would but work *deform* instead of *reform*" (AG 240).

"A Savior should be presented before the people, while the heart of the speaker should be *subdued* and *imbued* with His Spirit" (3T 32).

"At the time when the danger and depression of the church are greatest, the little company who are standing in the light will be *sighing* and *crying* for the abominations that are done in the land. But more especially will their prayers arise in behalf of the church because its members are doing after the manner of the world" (5T 209, 210).

‍‍‍‍ ‎

Personification: Projecting human life into abstractions; speaking of things as persons or attributing intelligence to inanimate objects or abstract ideas.

"There must be firmness in preserving order, but compassion, mercy, and forbearance should be mingled with the firmness. *Justice* has a *twin sister, Love.* These should stand side by side" (5T 559).

"You must remember that *Justice has a twin sister, Mercy.* When you would exercise justice, show mercy, tenderness, and love, and you will not labor in vain" (4T 363).

"*Justice* and *Mercy* are *twin sisters*, standing side by side" (4T 209).

"The long-suffering of God is wonderful. Long *does justice wait* while *mercy pleads* with the sinner" (COL 177).

"Long has *mercy extended a hand* of love, of patience and forbearance, toward a guilty world" (Mar 55).

"Amid the agonizing sufferings of the Son of God, blind and deluded men alone remain unfeeling. The chief priests and elders revile God's dear Son while in His expiring agonies. Yet inanimate *nature groans* in sympathy with *her* bleeding, dying Author. The earth trembles. The *sun refuses to behold* the scene. The heavens gather blackness. Angels have witnessed the scene of suffering until they can look no longer, and hide their faces from the horrid sight. Christ is dying!" (2T 209).

"*When Protestantism shall stretch her hand across the gulf to grasp the hand of the Roman power,* when she shall reach over the abyss to *clasp hands with spiritualism,* when, under the influence of this threefold union, our country shall repudiate every principle of its Constitution as a Protestant and republican government, . . . then we may know that the time has come for the marvelous working of Satan and that the end is near" (5T 451).

"The wind is boisterous. The waves roll high. . . . For a moment Christ is hidden from his view, and his faith gives way. He begins to sink. But while the *billows talk with death,* Peter lifts his eyes from the *angry waters,* and fixing them upon Jesus, cries, 'Lord, save me.' . . .
"When trouble comes upon us, how often we are like Peter! We look upon the waves, instead of keeping our eyes fixed upon the Savior. Our footsteps slide, and the *proud waters* go over our souls" (DA 381, 382).

"The massive [Jericho] *walls* of solid stone *frowned* darkly down, defying the siege of men" (4T 161).

"In the midst of the *angry heavens* is one clear space of indescribable glory, whence comes the voice of God" (GC 636).

<hr/>

Prolepsis: Speaking of a future event as though it has already taken place or is now taking place.

54

"Adam *is reinstated* in his first dominion. Transported with joy, he *beholds* the trees that were once his delight—the very trees whose fruit he himself had gathered in the days of his innocence and joy. He *sees* the vines that his own hands have trained, the very flowers that he once loved to care for. His mind *grasps* the reality of the scene; he *comprehends* that this *is* indeed Eden restored" (GC 648).

"It is at midnight that God *manifests* His power for the deliverance of His people. The sun *appears, shining* in its strength. Signs and wonders *follow* in quick succession. The wicked *look* with terror and amazement upon the scene, while the righteous *behold* with solemn joy the tokens of their deliverance. Everything in nature *seems* turned out of its course. The streams *cease* to flow. Dark, heavy clouds *come up and clash* against each other. In the midst of the angry heavens *is* one clear space of indescribable glory, whence *comes* the voice of God like the sound of many waters, saying: 'It is done.'. . . That voice *shakes* the heavens and the earth" (GC 636).

"The redeemed *raise* a song of praise that *echoes and reechoes* through the vaults of heaven: 'Salvation to our God which sitteth upon the throne, and unto the Lamb.' Verse 10 [Revelation 7]. And angel and seraph *unite* their voices in adoration" (GC 665).

"As they [the Jewish rulers] *gaze* upon His glory, there *flashes* before their minds the memory of the Son of Man clad in the garb of humanity. . . .

"They *behold* Him riding into Jerusalem, and *see* Him break into an agony of tears over the impenitent city that would not receive His message. His voice, which was heard in invitation, in entreaty, in tones of tender solicitude, *seems* again to fall upon their ears. The scene in the garden of Gethsemane *rises* before them, and they *hear* Christ's amazing prayer, 'Father, if it be possible, let this cup pass from me.'

"Again they *hear* the voice of Pilate, saying, 'I find in him no fault at all.' They *see* the shameful scene in the judgment hall, when Barabbas stood by the side of Christ, and they had the privilege of choosing the guiltless One. . . .

"Again they *see* their Sacrifice bearing the reproach of the cross. . . .

"Now they *behold* Him not in the garden of Gethsemane, not in the judgment hall, not on the cross of Calvary. The signs of His humiliation have passed away, and they *look* upon the face of God—the face they spit upon, the face which priests and rulers struck with the palms of their hands. Now the truth in all its vividness *is revealed* to them" (Mar 293).

"There *appears* against the sky a hand holding two tables of stone folded together. Says the prophet: 'The heavens shall declare his righteousness: for God is judge himself.' Psalm 50:6. That holy law, God's righteousness, that amid thunder and flame was proclaimed from Sinai as the guide of life, *is now* revealed to men as the rule of judgment. The hand *opens* the tables, and there *are seen* the precepts of the Decalogue, traced as with a pen of fire. The words *are* so plain that all can read them. Memory *is aroused*, the darkness of superstition and heresy *is swept* from every mind, and God's ten words, brief, comprehensive, and authoritative, *are presented* to the view of all the inhabitants of the earth" (GC 639).

ⵒⵛⵒ

Rhetorical question: Asking a question or series of questions that need no answer, and not waiting for an answer. Instead, the rhetorical question is posed for emphasis, effect, and even curiosity.

"Are there not many unpleasant pictures hanging in memory's halls? Often have you needed the forgiveness of Jesus. You have been constantly dependent upon His compassion and love. Yet have you not failed to manifest toward others the spirit which Christ has exercised toward you? Have you felt a burden for the one whom you saw venturing into forbidden paths? Have you kindly admonished him? Have you wept for him and prayed with him and for him? Have you shown by words of tenderness and kindly acts that you love him and desire to save him? As you have associated with those who were faltering and staggering under the load of their own infirmities of disposition and faulty habits, have you left them to fight the battles alone when you might have given them help? Have you not passed these sorely tempted ones by on the other side while the world has stood ready to give them sympathy and to allure them into Satan's nets? Have you not, like Cain, been ready to say: 'Am I my brother's keeper?' How must the great Head of the church regard the work of your life? How does He to whom every soul is precious, as the purchase of His blood, look upon your indifference to those who stray from the right path? Are you not afraid that He will leave you just as you leave them?" (5T 610, 611).

"Let the inquiry go forth from sincere hearts and trembling lips, 'Who shall be able to stand?' Have you, in these last precious hours of probation, been putting the very best material into your character building? Have you been purifying your souls from every stain? Have you followed the light? Have you works corresponding to your profession of faith?" (6T 405).

"You are bartering away the pearl of great price for present gain. While thus admonished of God, while in His providence He has, as it were, already placed your feet in the dark river, will you, dare you, cultivate your money-loving propensities? Will you, as the last act of a misspent life, overreach and retain that which is another's just due? Will you reason yourself into the belief that you are doing justice to your brother? Will you add another act of scheming and overreaching to those already written against you in the records above? Shall the blow of God's retributive judgment fall upon you and you be called without warning to pass through the dark waters?" (3T 545).

"You may each appropriately inquire: 'Why am I so slow to come out from the world and take Christ for my portion? Why should I love and honor those whom I know do not love God nor respect His claims? Why should I wish to retain the friendship of my Lord's enemies? Why should I follow their customs or be influenced by their opinions?' You cannot, my dear friends, serve both God and mammon" (5T 436).

⟨∽⟩

Simile: Comparison of different things or persons, usually introduced by "like" or "as."

"These wise men had seen the heavens illuminated with light, which enshrouded the heavenly host who heralded the advent of Christ to the humble shepherds. . . . This light was a distant cluster of flaming angels, which appeared *like a luminous star*" (Mar 11).

"Feeling the terrible power of temptation, . . . many a man cries in despair, 'I cannot resist evil.' Tell him that he can, that he must resist. . . . He is weak in moral power, controlled by the habits of a life of sin. His promises and resolutions are *like ropes of sand.* . . . But he need not despair" (MH 174, 175).

"A great name among men is *as letters traced in sand*, but a spotless character will endure to all eternity" (5T 579).

"*As one poor timber will sink a ship*, and *one flaw make a chain worthless*, so one demoralizing trait of character revealed in words or actions will leave its influence for evil, and if not overcome, will subvert every virtue" (4T 606).

"The heart that receives the Word of God is not *as a pool that evaporates*, not *like a broken cistern that loses its treasure.* It is *like the mountain stream*, fed by unfailing springs, whose cool, sparkling waters leap from rock to rock, refreshing the weary, the thirsty, the heavy-laden. It is *like a river constantly flowing* and, as it advances, becoming deeper and wider, until its life-giving waters are spread over all the earth. . . . So it is with the true child of God" (PK 233, 234).

"*But like the stars in the vast circuit of their appointed path*, God's purposes know no haste and no delay" (DA 32).

"When this change has been wrought in you, it will be as natural for you to live to bless others *as it is for the rosebush to yield its fragrant bloom*" (MB 128).

"While the members of the church are in a divided state of feeling, their hearts are hard and unimpressible. The efforts of the minister are *like blows upon cold iron*, and each party becomes more set in his own way than before" (5T 616).

"Some are uncourteous, abrupt, and harsh. They are *like chestnut burs*; they prick whenever touched. These do incalculable harm by misrepresenting our loving Savior" (5T 605).

"Brother E, your set positions and your strong, determined will to carry out your points at all hazards were felt and deplored by your wife, and her health suffered in consequence. . . . She was warped in her nature and could not act out herself. She *withered like a plant transplanted to an uncongenial soil*" (3T 463).

"Much hard labor is often expended that is not called for and that will never be appreciated. If those who have large concentrativeness cultivate this faculty to the neglect of others, they cannot have well-proportioned minds. They are *like machinery in which only one set of wheels works at a time.* While some wheels are rusting from inaction, others are wearing from constant use" (3T 35).

"When the noble and eloquent Stephen was stoned to death at the instigation of the Sanhedrin council, there was no loss to the cause of the gospel. The light of heaven that glorified his face, the divine compassion breathed in his dying prayer, were *as a sharp arrow of conviction* to the bigoted Sanhedrist who stood by, and Saul, the persecuting Pharisee, became a chosen vessel to bear the name of Christ before Gentiles and kings and the children of Israel" (MB 33, 34).

"Paul and Barnabas had learned to trust God's power to deliver. Their hearts were filled with fervent love for perishing souls. *As faithful shepherds in search of the lost sheep*, they gave no thought to their own ease and convenience" (AA 169).

⧼⧽

Synecdoche: Using part of something or someone to represent the whole object or the whole person.

"Jehoshaphat was a man of courage and valor. . . . He was well prepared to meet almost any foe; yet in this crisis he put not his trust in the *arm* of flesh. Not by disciplined armies and fenced cities, but by a living faith in the God of Israel, could he hope to gain the victory" (PK 198).

"Every child should be taught to show true reverence for God. Never should His name be spoken lightly or thoughtlessly. Angels, as they speak it, veil their faces. With what reverence should we, who are fallen and sinful, take it upon our *lips!*" (PK 236).

"It requires much study to know how to study. Each student must cultivate the habit of industry. He should see that no second-class work comes forth from his *hand*" (5T 524).

"The *feet* of the wicked will never desecrate the earth made new" (EW 52).

"The *arm* strong to smite the rebellious will be strong to deliver the loyal. Every faithful one will surely be gathered" (Mar 96).

"If men would reach the *ears* of the people in these days when pleasing fables are presented by eloquent *lips,* their minds must be disciplined and richly furnished with the imperishable truths of God's Word" (RH, April 6, 1886).

CHAPTER 4

MEMORY:

The Mind of the Sermon

As a part of the preaching process, *memory* includes—but is much broader than—word-for-word memorization of your message. The whole concept of memory takes in mental discipline and varying degrees of *familiarity* you have with your sermon material, as well as methods of preparation or methods of presentation commonly known as *manuscript, memory, extemporaneous,* and *impromptu.* Each one of these choices has both strengths and risks, so you will find yourself, through practice and experience, employing the one (or a combination of one or more) that best facilitates your preaching the Word of God.

Manuscript preaching is the writing out of your sermon word for word and essentially reading it at the moment of sharing with your congregation. One obvious advantage is the confidence from having right there before you your message in toto without fear of forgetting or leaving out something you had planned to say. A risk that tugs at this approach is your reading or your visible manuscript becoming a distraction and interfering with your communication.

Memory preaching (writing out the sermon and committing it to memory) generally frees you up to become more deliberate and connected with your audience, especially through eye contact and other interpersonal dynamics. One risk lies in the possibility of forgetting portions of the sermon, thus losing your planned organization and sequence.

Extemporaneous preaching usually wins more votes in its favor, because it combines just enough of *manuscript* and *memory* preaching to allow you their advantages without their pitfalls. For example, the *extemporaneous* sermon has notes and/or an outline (rather than a full manuscript), which provide sufficient material on paper for confidence and "safety" without the possible distraction of a full *manuscript* and minus having to rely on total recall demanded by the *memory* approach. You might say that the *extemporaneous* mode functions in the middle and helps to avoid what might be considered extremes of the other two modes.

Impromptu preaching, unlike the three methods mentioned above, really cannot be offered as a normal procedure of practice. The obvious reason is that by definition *impromptu* literally means "off the cuff" or "offhand" and refers to speaking "without advance knowledge or previous direct preparation." Although impromptu preaching may not qualify as a deliberately planned method of sermon preparation or presentation, it does serve a positive purpose in a backhanded way by opening the door of warning to all preachers to always be prepared "in season, out of season" (2 Timothy 4:2).

Again, the point must be emphasized that *memory* as a special consideration in homiletics transcends mere memorization of sermon material and embraces the whole range and sweep of mental discipline and continued growth for understanding and sharing the Word of God.

Preaching Principles of Ellen White on
Sermon Memory and *Preparation*

Mental discipline is necessary. "Those who teach the Word should not shun mental discipline. Every worker, or company of workers, should by persevering effort establish such rules and regulations as will lead to the formation of correct habits of thought and action. Such training is necessary not only for the young men but for the older workers, in order that their ministry may be free from mistakes, and their sermons be clear, accurate, and convincing" (Ev 648).

"Some of our ministers have a runway of discourses which they use year after year, with little variation. The illustrations are the same, and the words are almost the same. Such persons have ceased to improve, ceased to be students. They think to prevent mental decrepitude by not taxing the mind with too much study. Mistaken idea! It is only by being taxed that the mind gains vigor and acuteness. It must work, or it will lose its strength; it must have fresh subjects to feed upon, or it will starve. Unless it is made to think regularly and systematically, it will surely lose its power to think. . . . The mind must be made to penetrate beneath the surface" (RH, April 6, 1886).

Ministers should prayerfully study and memorize Scripture.

"Ministers should devote time to reading, to study, to meditation and prayer. They should store the mind with useful knowledge, committing to memory portions of Scripture, tracing out the fulfillment of the prophecies, and learning the lessons which Christ gave to His disciples" (4T 412).

Read in spare moments. "Take a book with you to read when traveling on the cars or waiting in the depot. Employ every spare moment in doing something" (4T 412).

Bible study requires thought and research. "The Bible is not studied as it should be. . . . Light reading fascinates the mind and makes the reading of God's Word uninteresting. . . . The Bible requires thought and prayerful research. It is not enough to skim over the surface. While some passages are too plain to be misunderstood, others are more intricate, demanding careful and patient study. Like the precious metal concealed in the hills and mountains, its gems of truth are to be searched out and stored in the mind for future use. Oh, that all would exercise their minds as constantly in searching for celestial gold as for the gold that perishes!" (4T 498, 499).

The truths of the Bible will be studied throughout eternity. "There are those in the ministry who have been readers of the Bible all their lives, and who think themselves so well versed in its teachings that they do not need to study it. Here is where they mistake. To the diligent Bible student new light, new ideas, new gems of truth, will constantly appear, and be eagerly grasped. Even through eternal ages the truths of this wonderful book will continue to unfold. . . .

"The gospel is not properly represented by those who have ceased to be students, who have, as it were, graduated in Bible study. If men would reach the ears of the people in these days when pleasing fables are presented by eloquent lips, their minds must be disciplined and richly furnished with the imperishable truths of God's Word" (RH, April 6, 1886).

Increase sermon subjects, storing truth in the mind. "Some who have been engaged in preaching for years are content to confine themselves to a few subjects, being too indolent to search the Scriptures diligently and prayerfully that they may become giants in the understanding of Bible doctrines and the practical lessons of Christ. The minds of all should be stored with a knowledge of the truths of God's Word, that they may be prepared, at any moment when required, to present from the storehouse things new and old. Minds have been crippled and dwarfed for want of zeal and of earnest, severe taxation. The time has come when God says: 'Go forward, and cultivate the abilities I have given you'" (4T 415).

Study yourself as well as your sermons. "If you were a devotional, godly man, in the pulpit and out, a mighty influence would attend your preaching. You do not closely search your own heart. You have studied many works to make your discourses thorough, able, and pleasing; but you have neglected the greatest and most necessary study, the study of yourself. A thorough knowledge of yourself, meditation and prayer, have come in as secondary things. Your success as a minister depends upon your keeping your own heart. You will receive more strength by spending one hour each day in meditation, and in mourning over your failings and heart corruptions and pleading for God's pardoning love and the assurance of sins forgiven, than you would by spending many hours and days in studying the most able authors, and making yourself acquainted with every objection to our faith, and with the most powerful evidences in its favor.

"The reason why our preachers accomplish so little is that they do not walk with God. He is a day's journey from most of them" (1T 433, 434).

Sermon preparation should leave room for God's leading. "Some ministers, in the preparation of their discourses, arrange every detail with such exactness that they give the Lord no room to lead their minds. Every point is fixed, stereotyped, as it were, and they seem unable to depart from the plan marked out. This is a grave error, and if followed, will cause ministers to become narrow-minded, and will leave them as destitute of spiritual life and energy as were the hills of Gilboa of dew and rain.

"When a minister feels that he cannot vary from a set discourse, the effect is little better than that produced by reading a sermon. Tame, formal discourses have in them very little of the vitalizing power of the Holy Spirit; and the habit of preaching such discourses will effectually destroy a minister's usefulness and ability. . . .

"Their hearts should be open, so that God may impress their minds, and then they will be able to give the people truth fresh from heaven. The Holy Spirit will give them ideas adapted to meet the needs of those present" (GW 165).

Satan seeks to block persons from coming to hear a sermon. "Like a skillful general he [Satan] lays his plans beforehand. As he sees the messenger of God searching the Scriptures, he takes note of the subject to be presented to the people. Then he employs all his cunning and shrewdness so to control circumstances that the message may not reach those whom he is deceiving on that very point. The one who most needs the warning will be urged into some business transaction which requires his presence, or will by some other means be prevented from hearing the words that might prove to him a savor of life unto life" (GC 518, 519).

Intellectual laziness is sin. "The intellect should be cultivated, the memory taxed. All intellectual laziness is sin, and spiritual lethargy is death. . . . Oh, that I could command language of sufficient force to make the impression I wish to make upon my fellow laborers in the gospel! My brethren, you are handling the words of life; you are dealing with minds that are capable of the highest development" (4T 399).

God encourages intellectual greatness. "God alone can measure the powers of the human mind. It was not His design that man should be content to remain in the lowlands of ignorance, but that he should secure all the advantages of an enlightened, cultivated intellect. Every man and every woman should feel that obligations are resting upon them to reach the very height of intellectual greatness" (4T 413).

The exercise of the mind increases mental strength and power. "He [a ministerial student] sees with intelligent eyes the perfection, knowledge, and wisdom of God stretching beyond into infinity. As his mind enlarges and expands, pure streams of light pour into his soul. The more he drinks from the fountain of knowledge, the purer and happier his contemplation of God's infinity, and the greater his longing for wisdom sufficient to comprehend the deep things of God.

"Mental culture is what we as a people need, and what we must have in order to meet the demands of the time. Poverty, humble origin, and unfavorable surroundings need not prevent the cultivation of the mind. The mental faculties must be kept under the control of the will and the mind not allowed to wander or become distracted with a variety of subjects at a time, being thorough in none. Difficulties will be met in all studies; but never cease through discouragement. Search, study, and pray; face every difficulty manfully and vigorously; call the power of will and the grace of patience to your aid, and then dig more earnestly till the gem of truth lies before you, plain and beautiful, all the more precious because of the difficulties involved in finding it. Do not, then, continually dwell upon this one point, concentrating all the energies of the mind upon it, constantly urging it upon the attention of others, but take another subject, and carefully examine that. Thus mystery after mystery will be unfolded to your comprehension. Two valuable victories will be gained by this course. You have not only secured useful knowledge, but the exercise of the mind has increased mental strength and power" (4T 414).

EWOP-3

CHAPTER 5

DELIVERY:

The Voice of the Sermon

In pulpit discourse, the moment of truth arrives when the preacher actually declares the message to the congregation. After all, everything done in earlier preparation was for the purpose of this precise time of interaction between pulpit and pew, speaker and assembled hearers. On the importance of *delivery,* the pendulum swings from persons who abhor attention to delivery and would soon ignore it to persons who insist that it must be studied and regarded as a tool or means rather than an end. To be sure, history has its examples of those who overplayed delivery, placing it above substance and content. Nevertheless, ample reason and support today consider delivery complementary to substance; and it is in this context that we encourage its consideration.

There are not a few students and practitioners of preaching who argue that this particular ingredient called *delivery* might be the most popular, if not the most important, activity of the preaching process. For sure, delivery can claim a certain prominence due to its occupying first chair, as it were, which enables the congregation to hear what is on the mind of the preacher or hear the answer to the question "Is there any word from the Lord?"

Cicero, one of the ancient teachers of rhetorical theory referred to earlier, can be counted among those who would rank delivery very high in the hierarchy of public address. Notice his bold and stark statement that carries endorsers even today: "Delivery, I say, has the sole and supreme power in oratory; without it, a speaker of the highest mental capacity can be held in no esteem; while one of moderate abilities, with this qualification, may surpass even those of the highest talent." The boldness of Cicero on this point is debatable for sure, but not to be totally ignored.

What do we mean by sermon delivery today? Surviving the years is the concept that oral delivery has two dimensions: (1) the visible code—that which influences the congregation from what it *sees* about the preacher; and (2) the audible code—that which influences the congregation from what it *hears* from the preacher.

Communication theory would urge that the moment that members of the audience visibly *see* the preacher, even sometimes a fairly long while before he or she begins speaking, they are already receiving positive and negative nonverbal messages from such general factors as posture (while the speaker is walking to the pulpit, sitting on the rostrum, or standing at the pulpit podium), dress, and bodily movements. More specific visible factors that influence audience response and preacher-listener interaction are gestures, eye contact, facial expression, personal involvement, enthusiasm, and even so-called stage fright or situational anxiety should the preacher display any evidence of unease and distracting nervousness.

Most often, sermon delivery focuses on vocalization (or "voice") of the speaker, that which the audience *hears*. We must understand, however, that the voice entails a package of specific features incorporating vocal volume, vocal pitch, vocal resonance, and vocal melody and rhythm, as well as the process of breathing and the element of time in speaking—all of which characterize and contribute to various qualities of vocal sound. Other important factors subsumed by vocalization are the clear production of words (pronunciation, articulation, and enunciation), correct grammar, and creative or symbolic language.

While preaching the gospel rightfully claims for itself a spiritual and divine activity, it also includes human and physiological dimensions in the light of God's utilizing the preacher as an "earthen vessel," thereby investing the sermon experience as another way that "the Word becomes flesh."

Preaching Principles of Ellen White on
Sermon Delivery

The grace of Christ energizes. "If you have the quickening grace of Christ to energize your movements, you will put earnestness into your sermons. Your subject will be clear and well-defined in your mind. You will not be lengthy in your remarks, neither will you speak hesitatingly, as though you did not yourself believe what you were saying. You must overcome slow hesitation, and undecided, sluggish movements, and learn to be minutemen" (VSS 217, 218).

Preachers must improve in pulpit manners. "The more closely a man walks with God, the more faultless will be his manner of address, his deportment, his attitude, and his gestures. Coarse and uncouth manners were never seen in our pattern, Christ Jesus. He was a representative of heaven, and His followers must be like Him" (GW 91).

Overcome defects in speaking. "No man should regard himself as qualified to enter the ministry until by persevering effort he has overcome every defect in his utterance. If he attempts to speak to the people without knowing how to use the talent of speech, half his influence is lost, for he has little power to hold the attention of a congregation.

"Whatever his calling, every person should learn to control the voice, so that when something goes wrong, he will not speak in tones that stir the worst passions of the heart. Too often the speaker and the one addressed speak sharply and harshly. Sharp, dictatorial words, uttered in hard, rasping tones, have separated friends and resulted in the loss of souls" (GW 87).

Speak clearly and plainly. "Students who expect to become workers in the cause of God should be trained to speak in a clear, straightforward manner, else they will be shorn of half their influence for good. The ability to speak plainly and clearly, in full, round tones, is invaluable in any line of work. This qualification is indispensable in those who desire to become ministers, evangelists, Bible workers, or canvassers. . . . The truth must not be marred by being communicated through defective utterance" (GW 86).

The apparel of the preacher is also a sermon. "The very dress will be a recommendation of the truth to unbelievers. It will be a sermon in itself. . . .

"A minister who is negligent in his apparel often wounds those of good taste and refined sensibilities. Those who are faulty in this respect should correct their errors and be more circumspect. The loss of some souls at last will be traced to the untidiness of the minister. The first appearance affected the people unfavorably because they could not in any way link his appearance with the truths he presented. His dress was against him; and the impression given was that the people whom he represented were a careless set who cared nothing abut their dress, and his hearers did not want anything to do with such a class of people. . . .

"Ministers sometimes stand in the desk with their hair in disorder, looking as if it had been untouched by comb and brush for a week. God is dishonored when those who engage in His sacred service are so neglectful of their appearance. Anciently the priests were required to have their garments in a particular style to do service in the holy place and minister in the priest's office. They were to have garments in accordance with their work, and God distinctly specified what these should be. . . .

"But look at the style of dress worn by some of our ministers at the present day" (2T 612-614).

Sermons are in everything pertaining to the preacher. "Our words, our actions, our deportment, our dress, everything, should preach. Not only with our words should we speak to the people, but everything pertaining to our person should be a sermon to them, that right impressions may be made upon them, and that the truth spoken may be taken by them to their homes. Thus our faith will stand in a better light before the community" (2T 618).

Preach with power and expression. "Ministers of the gospel should know how to speak with power and expression, making the words of eternal life so expressive and impressive that the hearers cannot but feel their weight. I am pained as I hear the defective voices of many of our ministers. Such ministers rob God of the glory He might have if they had trained themselves to speak the Word with power" (GW 87).

Cut preliminaries and apologies. "Many speakers waste their time and strength in long preliminaries and excuses. Some use nearly half an hour in making apologies; thus time is wasted, and when they reach their subject and try to fasten the points of truth in the minds of their hearers, the people are wearied out and cannot see their force.

"Instead of apologizing because he is about to address the people, the minister should begin as if he knew that he was bearing a message from God. He should make the essential points of truth as distinct as mileposts, so that the people cannot fail to see them" (GW 168).

Enthusiasm goes a long way. "The example of an energetic person is far-reaching; he has an electric power over others. He meets obstacles in his work; but he has the push in him, and instead of allowing his way to be hedged up, he breaks down every barrier.

"Especially should those who are engaged in teaching the Word of God cultivate a steady, unyielding energy in their labors. There are thorns in every path. All who follow the Lord's leading must expect to meet with disappointments, crosses, and losses. But a spirit of true heroism will help them to overcome these" (RH, April 6, 1886).

Don't preach without feeling. "Is not too much at stake to preach in an indifferent manner and without feeling the burden of souls? In this age of moral darkness it will take something more than dry theory to move souls. Ministers must have a living connection with God. They must preach as though they believed what they said" (4T 447).

Avoid long sermons. "Long discourses and tedious prayers are positively injurious to a religious interest and fail to carry conviction to the consciences of the people. This propensity for speechmaking frequently dampens a religious interest that might have produced great results" (4T 261).

Short messages are preferred. "Let the message for this time be presented, not in long, labored discourses, but in short talks, right to the point. Lengthy sermons tax the strength of the speaker and the patience of his hearers. If the speaker is one who feels the importance of his message, he will need to be especially careful lest he overtax his physical powers, and give the people more than they can remember" (GW 167, 168).

Read with a soft, musical cadence. "The one who gives Bible readings in the congregation or in the family should be able to read with a soft, musical cadence which will charm the hearers" (GW 87).

Fluent delivery is to be undergirded by spiritual power. "Brother B's preaching has not been marked by the sanction of God's Spirit. He can talk fluently and make a point plain, but his preaching has lacked spirituality. His appeals have not touched the heart with a new tenderness. There has been an array of words, but the hearts of his hearers have not been quickened and melted with a sense of a Savior's love. Sinners have not been convicted and drawn to Christ by a sense that 'Jesus of Nazareth passeth by.' Sinners should have a clear impression given them of the nearness and willingness of Christ to give them present salvation. A Savior should be presented before the people, while the heart of the speaker should be subdued and imbued with His Spirit. The very tones of the voice, the look, the words, should possess an irresistible power to move hearts and control minds. Jesus should be found in the heart of the minister. If Jesus is in the words and in the tones of the voice, if they are mellow with His tender love, it will prove a blessing of more value than all the riches, pleasures, and glories of the earth; for such blessings will not come and go without accomplishing a work. Convictions will be deepened, impressions will be made, and the question will be raised: 'What shall I do to be saved?'" (3T 31, 32).

Practice articulation and voice control. "Ministers and teachers should discipline themselves to articulate clearly and distinctly, allowing the full sound to every word. Those who talk rapidly, from the throat, jumbling the words together, and raising the voice to an unnaturally high pitch, soon become hoarse, and the words spoken lose half the force which they would have if spoken slowly, distinctly, and not so loud. The sympathies of the hearers are awakened for the speaker; for they know that he is doing violence to himself, and they fear that he will break down at any moment. It is no evidence that a man has zeal for God because he works himself up into a frenzy of excitement and gesticulation. 'Bodily exercise,' says the apostle, 'profiteth little'" (GW 91).

Ministers should model good posture, correct breathing, and healthful physical practices. "Some of our most talented ministers are doing themselves great injury by their defective manner of speaking. While teaching the people their duty to obey God's moral law, they should not be found violating the laws of God in regard to health and life. Ministers should stand erect, and speak slowly, firmly, and distinctly, taking a full inspiration of air at every sentence, and throwing out the words by exercising the abdominal muscles. If they will observe this simple rule, giving attention to the laws of health in others respects, they may preserve their life and usefulness much longer than men in any other profession. The chest will become broader, and . . . the speaker need seldom become hoarse, even by constant speaking. Instead of becoming consumptives, ministers may, by exercising care, overcome all tendency to consumption.

"Unless ministers educate themselves to speak in accordance with physical law, they will sacrifice life, and many will mourn the loss of 'those martyrs to the cause of truth,' when the facts in the case are, that by indulging in wrong habits, they did injustice to themselves and to the truth which they represented, and robbed God and the world of the service they might have rendered. God would have been pleased to have them live, but they slowly committed suicide" (GW 90).

Compare the voice of Jesus to the voice of some preachers today. "Jesus uttered truth in a plain, direct manner, giving vital force and impressiveness to all His utterances. Had He raised His voice to an unnatural key, as is customary with many preachers in this day, the pathos and melody of the human voice would have been lost, and much of the force of the truth destroyed" (Ev 56).

Avoid loud and hurried preaching. "From the light I have had, the ministry is a sacred and exalted office, and those who accept this position should have Christ in their hearts and manifest an earnest desire to represent Him worthily before the people in all their acts, in their dress, in their speaking, and even in their manner of speaking. They should speak with reverence. Some destroy the solemn impression they may have made upon the people by raising their voices to a very high pitch and hallooing and screaming out the truth. When presented in this manner, truth loses much of its sweetness, its force and solemnity. But if the voice is toned right, if it has solemnity, and is so modulated as to be even pathetic, it will produce a much better impression. This was the tone in which Christ taught His disciples. He impressed them with solemnity; He spoke in a pathetic manner. But this loud hallooing—what does it do? It does not give the people any more exalted views of the truth and does not impress them any more deeply. It only causes a disagreeable sensation to the hearers and wears out the vocal organs of the speaker. The tones of the voice have much to do in affecting the hearts of those that hear.

"Many who might be useful men are using up their vital force and destroying their lungs and vocal organs by their manner of speaking. Some ministers have acquired a habit of hurriedly rattling off what they have to say as though they had a lesson to repeat and were hastening through it as fast as possible. This is not the best manner of speaking. By using proper care, every minister can educate himself to speak distinctly and impressively, not to hurriedly crowd the words together without taking time to breathe. He should speak in a moderate manner, that the people may get the ideas fixed in their minds as he passes along. But when the matter is rushed through so rapidly, the people cannot get the points in their minds, and they do not have time to receive the impression that it is important for them to have; nor is there time for the truth to affect them as it otherwise would.

"Speaking from the throat, letting the words come out from the upper extremity of the vocal organs, all the time fretting and irritating them, is not the best way to preserve health or to increase the efficiency of those organs. You should take a full inspiration and let the action come from the abdominal muscles. Let the lungs be only the channel, but do not depend upon them to do the work. If you let your words come from deep down, exercising the abdominal muscles, you can speak to thousands with just as much ease as you can speak to ten.

"Some of our preachers are killing themselves by long, tedious praying and loud speaking, when a lower tone would make a better impression and save their own strength. Now, while you go on regardless of the laws of life and health, and follow the impulse of the moment, do not charge it upon God if you break down. . . .

"There is another class that address the people in a whining tone. Their hearts are not softened by the Spirit of God, and they think they must make an impression by the appearance of humility. But such a course does not exalt the gospel ministry, but brings it down and degrades it. Ministers should present the truth warm from glory. They should speak in such a manner as rightly to represent Christ and preserve the dignity becoming His ministers. . . .

"A mistake has been made by many in their religious exercises in long praying and long preaching, upon a high key, with a forced voice, in an unnatural strain and an unnatural tone. The minister has needlessly wearied himself and really distressed the people by hard, labored exercise, which is all unnecessary. Ministers should speak in a manner to reach and impress the people. The teachings of Christ were impressive and solemn; His voice was melodious. And should not we, as well as Christ, study to have melody in our voices? He had a mighty influence, for He was the Son of God. We are so far beneath Him and so far deficient, that, do the very best we can, our efforts will be poor. We cannot gain and possess the influence that He had; but why should we not educate ourselves to come just as near to the Pattern as it is possible for us to do, that we may have the greatest possible influence upon the people?" (2T 615-618).

Proper vocal delivery can be a matter of life and death. "Brother D . . . should avoid lengthy preaching and long prayers. These are no benefit to himself or to others. Long and violent exercise of the vocal organs has irritated his throat and lungs, and injured his general health, more than his precise rounds of rules for eating and resting have benefited him. One overexertion or strain of the vocal organs may not soon be recovered from, and may cost the life of the speaker. A calm, unhurried, yet earnest, manner of speaking will have a better influence upon a congregation than to let the feelings become excited and control the voice and manners. As far as possible the speaker should preserve the natural tones of the voice. It is the truth presented that affects the heart. If the speaker makes these truths a reality, he will, with the aid of the Spirit of God, be able to impress the hearers with the fact that he is in earnest, without straining the fine organs of the throat or the lungs" (2T 672).

Jesus demonstrated a wide range of qualities in His delivery. "His voice was as music to those who had listened to the monotonous tones of the rabbis. . . . The rabbis spoke with doubt and hesitancy, as if the Scriptures might be interpreted to mean one thing or exactly the opposite. The hearers were daily involved in greater uncertainty. But Jesus taught the Scriptures as of unquestionable authority. . . .

"Yet He was earnest, rather than vehement. He spoke as one who had a definite purpose to fulfill. . . .

73

"The beauty of His countenance, the loveliness of His character, above all, the look expressed in look and tone, drew to Him all who were not hardened in unbelief. Had it not been for the sweet, sympathetic spirit that shone out in every look and word, He would not have attracted the large congregations that He did. . . .

"Jesus watched with deep earnestness the changing countenances of His hearers. The faces that expressed interest and pleasure gave Him great satisfaction. As the arrows of truth pierced to the soul, breaking through the barriers of selfishness, and working contrition, and finally gratitude, the Savior was made glad. When His eye swept over the throng of listeners, and He recognized among them the faces He had before seen, His countenance lighted up with joy. He saw in them hopeful subjects for His kingdom. When the truth, plainly spoken, touched some cherished idol, He marked the changed countenance, the cold, forbidding look, which told that the light was unwelcome. When He saw men refuse the message of peace, His heart was pierced to the very depths" (DA 253-255).

Jesus' voice and gestures had impact. "The words of life were presented in such simplicity that a child could understand them. Men, women, and children were so impressed with His manner of explaining the Scriptures that they would catch the very intonation of His voice, place the same emphasis on their words, and imitate His gestures. Youth caught His spirit of ministry and sought to pattern after His gracious ways by seeking to assist those whom they saw needing help" (CH 498, 499).

Jesus' facial expression gave meaning to His words. "When Jesus delivered the Sermon on the Mount, His disciples were gathered close about Him, and the multitude, filled with intense curiosity, also pressed as near as possible. Something more than usual was expected. Eager faces and listening attitudes gave evidence of the deep interest. The attention of all seemed riveted upon the speaker. His eyes were lighted up with unutterable love, and the heavenly expression upon His countenance gave meaning to every word uttered" (5T 253).

CHAPTER 6

THE SIXTH CANON:

After the Sermon Is Over

Could it be possible that all the energy, time, and thought devoted to sermon preparation and proclamation have an ultimate goal *beyond the pulpit?* Is there really more to be done? Cannot I enjoy the satisfaction of having completed my preaching task when my final words for that particular discourse have been spoken? Well, yes and no.

Let us say that the sermon was a joy to put together because everything fell into place during my sermon development. Also, it was a profound joy to present to the waiting congregation; their response and acceptance proved encouraging during both the message and the appeal, with a number of persons surrendering their lives to Jesus Christ as Savior and Lord.

So what is there left for the preacher beyond this? For sure, the sermon experience itself must never be downplayed. It will always be central and crucial. But after having delivered the message, that becomes a thing of the past. Furthermore, the preacher must not fall into the trap of resting on his or her laurels following a good sermon. As a matter of fact, it is high time to begin thinking about the *next* sermon to be prepared and preached.

Nevertheless, according to Ellen White, after the preaching of every sermon there remains something else besides just another discourse. Her following counsel challenges each of us to become the complete preacher beyond sermon concerns, yes, *beyond the pulpit.*

Principles of Ellen White on
Being Complete Preachers

Ministry involves personal labor. "Ministry means much more than sermonizing; it means earnest personal labor" (GW 185).

Ministers should visit people. "When a minister has presented the gospel message from the pulpit, his work is only begun. There is personal work for him to do. He should visit the people in their homes, talking and praying with them in earnestness and humility" (GW 187).

Live out your preaching. "When they preach from the desk, they only commence their work. They must then live out their preaching, ever guarding themselves, that they bring not a reproach upon the cause of God. They should illustrate by example the life of Christ. 1 Corinthians 3:9: 'For we are labourers together with God.' 2 Corinthians 6:1: 'We then, as workers together with Him, beseech you also that ye receive not the grace of God in vain.' The minister's work is not done when he leaves the desk. He should not then throw off the burden and occupy his mind with reading or writing unless this is actually necessary. He should follow up his public labors by private efforts, laboring personally for souls whenever an opportunity presents, conversing around the fireside, beseeching and entreating souls in Christ's stead to be reconciled to God" (1T 432).

Imprudent actions can counteract powerful sermons. "Godly men, faithful, holy men, who carry out in their everyday life that which they preach, will exert a saving influence. A powerful discourse delivered from the desk may affect minds; but a little imprudence upon the part of the minister out of the pulpit, a lack of gravity of speech and true godliness, will counteract his influence, and do away the good impressions made by him. The converts will be his; in many instances they will seek to rise no higher than their preacher. . . .

"The success of a minister depends much upon his deportment out of the desk. When he ceases preaching and leaves the desk, his work is not finished; it is only commenced. He must then carry out what he has preached" (1T 380).

Become acquainted with your hearers. "The minister's work is but just begun when he has presented the truth from the pulpit. He is then to become acquainted with his hearers. Many greatly fail in not coming in close sympathy with those who most need their help. With the Bible in their hand they should seek in a courteous manner to learn the objections which exist in the minds of those who are beginning to inquire: 'What is truth?'" (4T 263).

Unselfish effort speaks loudly. "Personal, unselfish effort will accomplish more for the cause of Christ than can be wrought by sermons or creeds" (GW 200).

The love of Christ wins souls. "Their hearts may be as hard as the beaten highway, and apparently it may be a useless effort to present the Savior to them; but while logic may fail to move, and argument be powerless to convince, the love of Christ, revealed in personal ministry, may soften the stony heart, so that the seed of truth can take root" (GW 185).

Don't renounce social communion. "The example of Christ in linking Himself with the interests of humanity should be followed by all who preach His Word, and by all who have received the gospel of His grace. We are not to renounce social communion. We should not seclude ourselves from others. In order to reach all classes, we must meet them where they are. They will seldom seek us of their own accord. Not alone from the pulpit are the hearts of men touched by divine truth. There is another field of labor, humbler, it may be, but fully as promising. It is found in the home of the lowly, and in the mansion of the great; at the hospitable board, and in gatherings for innocent social enjoyment" (DA 152).

Final Word

So then, preachers, hopefully these pages have whetted your appetite to continue exploring the inspired counsel of Ellen G. White on the glorious task of proclaiming the gospel of Jesus Christ. Preaching is like a crimson ribbon threading itself through pulpit, pew, and continuous personal interaction. Your sermons will accomplish their best purpose when you are responsibly interpreting the biblical story, relevantly applying the message, and resolutely maintaining a meaningful relation with hearers who respond to the atoning love of Calvary.

To fulfill the gospel commission, the spoken word forever lives between the mountain and the multitude and, in the poignant words of Karl Barth, attains perpetual relevance when proceeding "with the Bible in one hand and the newspaper in the other." If the good news of salvation is the best that God has to offer humankind, then you and I should bring our best to this task so that the grace of God might accomplish its best.

No one understood this imperative or penned it or preached it more clearly and passionately than Ellen Gould Harmon White. In the authority that only heaven can bestow, let us, therefore, "Go into all the world and preach the good news to all creation. Whoever believes and is baptized will be saved" (Mark 16:15, 16, NIV).

INDEX